The Choctaw

Indians of North America

Heritage Edition

◄Indians ►
◄of North►
◄America ►

Heritage Edition

Indians of North America

The Choctaw

Jesse O. McKee

Foreword by
Ada E. Deer
University of Wisconsin-Madison

CHELSEA HOUSE
PUBLISHERS
A Haights Cross Communications Company

Philadelphia

COVER: Beaded bandolier with powderhorn, early nineteenth century.

CHELSEA HOUSE PUBLISHERS

VP, NEW PRODUCT DEVELOPMENT   Sally Cheney
DIRECTOR OF PRODUCTION   Kim Shinners
CREATIVE MANAGER   Takeshi Takahashi
MANUFACTURING MANAGER   Diann Grasse

Staff for THE CHOCTAW

EXECUTIVE EDITOR   Lee Marcott
EDITOR   Christian Green
PRODUCTION EDITOR   Noelle Nardone
PHOTO EDITOR   Sarah Bloom
SERIES AND COVER DESIGNER   Keith Trego
LAYOUT   21st Century Publishing and Communications, Inc.

A Haights Cross Communications ✈ Company

www.chelseahouse.com

First Printing

9 8 7 6 5 4 3 2 1

Library of Congress Cataloging-in-Publication Data

McKee, Jesse O.
   The Choctaw / Jesse O. McKee.
      p. cm.—(Indians of North America)
Includes bibliographical references and index.
   ISBN 0-7910-7994-5 — ISBN 0-7910-8348-9 (pbk.)
   1. Choctaw Indians. I. Title. II. Indians of North America (Chelsea House Publishers)
E99.C8M36 2004
976.004'97387—dc22

                                                         2004004629

Contents

Foreword

Ada E. Deer

American Indians are an integral part of our nation's life and history. Yet most Americans think of their Indian neighbors as stereotypes; they are woefully uninformed about them as fellow humans. They know little about the history, culture, and contributions of Native people. In this new millennium, it is essential for every American to know, understand, and share in our common heritage. The Cherokee teacher, the Mohawk steelworker, and the Ojibwe writer all express their tribal heritage while living in mainstream America.

The revised INDIANS OF NORTH AMERICA series, which focuses on some of the continent's larger tribes, provides the reader with an accurate perspective that will better equip him/her to live and work in today's world. Each tribe has a unique history and culture, and knowledge of individual tribes is essential to understanding the Indian experience.

Prior to the arrival of Columbus in 1492, scholars estimate the Native population north of the Rio Grande ranged from seven to twenty-five million people who spoke more than three hundred different languages. It has been estimated that ninety percent of the Native population was wiped out by disease, war, relocation, and starvation. Today there are more than 567 tribes, which have a total population of more than two million. When Columbus arrived in the Bahamas, the Arawak Indians greeted him with gifts, friendship, and hospitality. He noted their ignorance of guns and swords and wrote they could easily be overtaken with fifty men and made to do whatever he wished. This unresolved clash in perspectives continues to this day.

A holistic view recognizing the connections of all people, the land, and animals pervades the life and thinking of Native people. These core values—respect for each other and all living things; honoring the elders; caring, sharing, and living in balance with nature; and using not abusing the land and its resources—have sustained Native people for thousands of years.

American Indians are recognized in the U.S. Constitution. They are the only group in this country who has a distinctive *political* relationship with the federal government. This relationship is based on the U.S. Constitution, treaties, court decisions, and attorney-general opinions. Through the treaty process, millions of acres of land were ceded *to* the U.S. government *by* the tribes. In return, the United States agreed to provide protection, health care, education, and other services. All 377 treaties were broken by the United States. Yet treaties are the supreme law of the land as stated in the U.S. Constitution and are still valid. Treaties made more than one hundred years ago uphold tribal rights to hunt, fish, and gather.

Since 1778, when the first treaty was signed with the Lenni-Lenape, tribal sovereignty has been recognized and a government-to-government relationship was established. This concept of tribal power and authority has continuously been misunderstood by the general public and undermined by the states. In a series of court decisions in the 1830s, Chief Justice John Marshall described tribes as "domestic dependent nations." This status is not easily understood by most people and is rejected by state governments who often ignore and/or challenge tribal sovereignty. Sadly, many individual Indians and tribal governments do not understand the powers and limitations of tribal sovereignty. An overarching fact is that Congress has plenary, or absolute, power over Indians and can exercise this sweeping power at any time. Thus, sovereignty is tenuous.

Since the July 8, 1970, message President Richard Nixon issued to Congress in which he emphasized "self-determination without termination," tribes have re-emerged and have utilized the opportunities presented by the passage of major legislation such as the American Indian Tribal College Act (1971), Indian Education Act (1972), Indian Education and Self-Determination Act (1975), American Indian Health Care Improvement Act (1976), Indian Child Welfare Act (1978), American Indian Religious Freedom Act (1978), Indian Gaming Regulatory Act (1988), and Native American Graves Preservation and Repatriation Act (1990). Each of these laws has enabled tribes to exercise many facets of their sovereignty and consequently has resulted in many clashes and controversies with the states and the general public. However, tribes now have more access to and can afford attorneys to protect their rights and assets.

Under provisions of these laws, many Indian tribes reclaimed power over their children's education with the establishment of tribal schools and thirty-one tribal colleges. Many Indian children have been rescued from the foster-care system. More tribal people are freely practicing their traditional religions. Tribes with gaming revenue have raised their standard of living with improved housing, schools, health clinics, and other benefits. Ancestors' bones have been reclaimed and properly buried. All of these laws affect and involve the federal, state, and local governments as well as individual citizens.

Tribes are no longer people of the past. They are major players in today's economic and political arenas; contributing millions of dollars to the states under the gaming compacts and supporting political candidates. Each of the tribes in INDIANS OF NORTH AMERICA demonstrates remarkable endurance, strength, and adaptability. They are buying land, teaching their language and culture, and creating and expanding their economic base, while developing their people and making decisions for future generations. Tribes will continue to exist, survive, and thrive.

Ada E. Deer
University of Wisconsin-Madison
June 2004

1

Choctaw Origins

The *Choctaws* are great storytellers. They have two stories of their origin, which they have passed down orally from generation to generation for many centuries. One story maintains that the Choctaws first lived somewhere in what is now the western United States and then migrated to present-day Mississippi. Although the story does not fully explain why the *tribe* left the West, some versions suggest that either the Choctaws' first homeland had become overpopulated or that they wished to escape constant warfare with neighboring tribes. Carrying the bones of their ancestors, the Choctaws journeyed eastward, a course indicated by a sacred pole that their leader, Chata, placed in the ground at the end of each day's journey. Every morning, they found that the pole was leaning toward the east and set off in that direction, led by a white dog with magical powers that slept at the base of the pole each night. For months, the Choctaws wandered, crossing a great river (the Mississippi) and continuing east. Finally, one morning, they found that the dog had died and that the pole was standing upright. The Choctaws took this as a sign that they had at last arrived in their new homeland.

To celebrate the occasion, the Choctaws built a large *mound* in which they buried their ancestors' remains. Because the mound was slanted, they called it *Nanih Waiya*, or "leaning mound." This great oblong structure, located in what is today southern Winston County in east-central Mississippi, stood nearly forty feet high with a base of approximately one acre and a summit of about one-fourth of an acre. The Choctaws fortified the mound with an eight-foot-high circular wall measuring one and a half to two miles in circumference. Archaeologists believe that the mound was the location for political and religious meetings of the tribe from about 500 B.C. until the arrival of Europeans in the area in the early 1700s A.D.

The Choctaws' second story of their origin states that they were created in the center of Nanih Waiya by a great spirit and then they crawled to the surface of the earth through a hole in the ground or a cave. In another version of this creation story, the Creek, Cherokee, and Chickasaw Indians came out of the mound before the Choctaws finally emerged. The other groups migrated to neighboring areas, but when the Choctaws surfaced, they dried themselves in the sun, looked around, and chose to settle on the land surrounding Nanih Waiya. (For additional information on this sacred Choctaw site, enter "Nanih Waiya Mound" into any search engine and browse the many sites listed.)

The early Choctaws left no written records of the way they lived, but archaeologists and other scholars have learned much about the Choctaws' *prehistory* from studying *artifacts*— handmade objects they left behind, such as projectile points (arrowheads or spear points) and pottery. The written observations of the European explorers and travelers who visited the area as early as the sixteenth century also contribute information about prehistoric Choctaw life.

Nanih Waiya, which is located in southern Winston County in east-central Mississippi, is a rectangular platform mound that is venerated by the Choctaws. One of the Choctaws' creation stories holds that they were the last of four tribes to emerge from the ground beneath Nanih Waiya. The other tribes—the Cherokee, Chickasaw, and Creek—went their separate ways, but the Choctaw decided to settle in the area of Nanih Waiya.

The region that the early Choctaws inhabited (now the states of Mississippi, western Alabama, and eastern Louisiana) has a warm, moist climate with mild winters, hot summers, and ample rainfall. The area is covered with low, rolling hills blanketed with pine trees, and hardwoods are found along the many creeks and rivers that flow through the land. The forests provided the Choctaws with firewood and building materials, and the wild plants, game, and fish that were abundant in the region provided much of their food.

Although the soil was not extremely rich, Choctaw men, women, and children cultivated the river *floodplains*. All Choctaw land was held in common by the tribe, but individuals had a claim to any tract they cultivated as long as they did not encroach upon fields that were already claimed by other Choctaws. If a Choctaw abandoned his or her field, control over it reverted to the tribe.

The Choctaws cleared their fields in midwinter by burning the underbrush and killing the trees by cutting off a ring of bark near the base of their trunks. In the spring, they planted corn (maize)—their most important crop—as well as beans, melons, pumpkins, peas, squash, sweet potatoes, and sunflowers. The tribe's farming tools included spades and shovels made from cedarwood and hoes constructed from pieces of flint, the bones of an animal, such as the shoulder blades of a bison, or bent sticks.

When the men were not working in the fields, they fished and hunted wild game, which provided the Choctaws with much of their food. Hunting parties stalked deer, bear, bison, turkey, squirrel, otter, beaver, raccoon, and rabbit, and killed their prey with bows and arrows, axes, knives, and tomahawks. Aside from being the tribe's main source of meat, deer and bears gave the Choctaws skins, which they made into clothing and moccasins. They also created ornaments and necklaces from bear claws and from bone fragments of other animals, and they cooked their food and groomed their hair and bodies with oil found in bear fat.

Boys, and sometimes girls, joined hunting expeditions close to the fields. Early in life, they were taught to recognize the tracks of small animals, which they hunted with blowguns made of seven-foot-long reeds. After loading an arrowhead into the reed, children would aim it at their prey and then shoot the arrowhead by blowing into the pipe. As boys grew older, their male elders taught them good sportsmanship and hunting skills, such as how to track and locate larger animals and how to use a bow and arrow. Men also trained boys for bow-and-arrow competitions, which were popular among the Choctaws.

Children, women, and the elderly added to the food supply by gathering wild plants, fruits, and nuts in tall grass baskets. Hickory nuts, pecans, walnuts, chestnuts, and acorns were especially important to the tribe. Women, who were responsible for all food preparation, often mixed nuts with water, combined them with vegetables or breads, or used them for stews, oil, and drinks.

The main ingredient of many of the Choctaws' favorite dishes was corn, which they used to make grits, hominy, porridge, and meal. Choctaw women also pounded boiled corn (*tafula*) and frequently mixed it with beans. Another popular dish, *bunaha*, consisted of pounded cornmeal combined with boiled beans. The Choctaws wrapped this dough in corn husks, then boiled the husks and set them aside until they needed the cooked bunaha.

The Choctaws paid a great deal of attention to their clothing and ornaments. Men always wore a belt and a loincloth. In the winter, they also put on leggings and moccasins and wore garments on their upper torsos that were woven from feathers or the bark of mulberry trees. Women wore short skirts of deerskin, but when the weather was cold, they also wrapped themselves in deerskin shawls and put on moccasins. Both men and women often wore brightly colored ornaments made from nuts, bones, stones, and seeds and sometimes placed feathers in their hair.

The early Choctaws built their homes from a wood frame made of posts fastened together with vines. They plastered the interior with mud, which dried in the sun to form windowless walls. The Choctaws then covered the outside with the bark of cypress or pine trees. The single door was only about three to four feet high. Because the Choctaws built fires in the middle of their dwellings for heat and cooking, they left a hole at the top of two opposite walls to let the smoke out. The most-used furnishings in their homes were platforms woven from cane, which served as beds, tables, and seats. Skins of bears, deer, or bison (buffalo) were used for blankets, and sun-baked earthen pots and pans for cooking.

Most Choctaws lived in villages, which were located within three geographic divisions: *Okla Falaya* (long people), to the northwest; *Okla Tannap*, or *Ahepat Okla* (people of the opposite side), to the northeast; and *Okla Hannali* (people of Six Towns), to the south. For most of their prehistory, the Choctaws probably lived solely in these three districts, but there may have once been a small, fourth division, called *Okla Chito* (big people), in the center of the Choctaw domain.

Each of the three divisions grew up around one of their land's three major rivers—the Pearl, the Tombigbee, and the Pascagoula, respectively—and the rivers' tributaries. There were slight variations in the dress and speech among the inhabitants of the three divisions, but more significant were the different alliances and trade relations between each division and the neighboring tribes geographically closest to it. Okla Falaya had strong ties to the Chakchiuma and Chickasaw tribes to the west; Okla Tannap, to the Alabama to the east; and Okla Hannali, to smaller Indian groups, such as the Mobile, to the south.

Each geographic division was governed by a *mingo* or district chief. A mingo was elected by the men within his district and was usually a man from an influential family with demonstrated leadership ability. Each village also had its own chief to preside over meetings of a council composed of village elders. Village chiefs were aided by four or five assistants, who often helped them predict the future. One of the assistants was a war chief who was in charge of all military matters.

When it was necessary, a mingo would call for a council of all village chiefs in his division. The three district chiefs, who together governed the affairs of the entire tribal *nation*, sometimes called for a national council composed of the members of all three district councils. Council decisions had to be supported by a majority of the meeting's participants. Thus, with its election of officials, civilian rule, and unlimited opportunity

The Choctaws lived in three districts—Okla Falaya, Okla Tannap, and Okla Hannali—
that were largely centered along rivers. This painting details a Choctaw encampment
along the Mississippi River, which was the western border of the Okla Falaya District.

for issues to be debated, the Choctaw system of government was, in many respects, very democratic.

Socially, the Choctaws were separated into two divisions, each of which contained six to eight *clans*. Division membership had great significance. For instance, marriage between members of the same division or the same clan was prohibited. Because the Choctaws were *matrilineal*, meaning that they traced descent through the female side of the family, children belonged to their mother's clan, while their father was a member of the clan of his own mother. If parents were separated, the offspring always remained with the mother.

Choctaw children were raised in an atmosphere of relative freedom. A mother was responsible for the upbringing of her daughters. A mother's brothers, however, took charge of raising her sons because they were the closest male relatives who—unlike the father—were members of the boys' clan. Maternal uncles disciplined and trained boys in hunting, warfare, and ball playing. If a boy was disobedient, an older man often punished him, first with a scolding and then by pouring cold water on the boy.

Children were frequently named after some event that occurred at the time they were born. Later in life, a Choctaw was given another name as a result of some adventure, exploit, or personal characteristic. A speech or ceremony sometimes accompanied the granting of this second name.

Although the early Choctaws conducted few ceremonies, singing and dancing were a part of their everyday life, and they held feasts regularly. Among the most important dances the Choctaws performed were the *Green Corn Dance,* held in the late summer in anticipation of the corn harvest; the War Dance, performed before military expeditions; and the Ball-Play Dance, done on nights before the Choctaws played *ishtaboli,* the tribe's favorite ball game. The Choctaws held other less-significant dances to honor various birds and animals, such as the turkey, bison, and bear. The Choctaws usually performed these dances in an open space in the center of each village to the beat of a drum. To make a drum, a Choctaw would cut a section from the trunk of a small hollow tree and stretch a fresh deerskin over the opening. When the skin dried, it became tight. They then played the instrument by hitting the hide with a stick.

One of the recreational activities the Choctaws enjoyed most was playing ishtaboli, a ball game similar to the sport we know today as lacrosse. At the start of the game, the players, divided into two teams, would gather at the center of a large field with goals at each end. A judge would then toss a small leather ball into the air, which the players would chase, trying to hit it across the field with their two rackets, called *kapuchas.* The objective was to hit the ball into the opponents' goal.

The game was over when one team had scored a set number of goals, usually ten or twenty.

Ishtaboli was a social event involving men and women, both young and old. Most games were played between different villages or against a neighboring tribe, usually with seventy-five to one hundred players to a team. Although the Choctaws

(continued on page 12)

A Game of Ishtaboli

George Catlin was born in Wilkes-Barre, Pennsylvania, in 1796. He attended law school and practiced as an attorney before deciding to pursue his first love, painting. He quickly became a noted portraitist in Philadelphia and received commissions to paint a number of prominent people, among them President James Monroe, former President James Madison, and Madison's wife, Dolley. In the late 1820s, Catlin visited several nearby Indian reservations, where he painted members of the Seneca, Oneida, Ottawa, and Mohegan tribes.

Fascinated by these tribespeople and their ways of life, Catlin left Philadelphia in 1830, journeying west in order to observe and paint other tribes and their villages. For six years, Catlin journeyed up the Mississippi and Missouri Rivers and over the plains of the Southwest, visiting some forty-eight tribes and capturing their daily lives in hundreds of paintings. These works, combined with the journal Catlin kept during his travels, constitute one of the most comprehensive eyewitness records of the Indians on the American frontier.

Catlin visited the Choctaw Nation in the summer of 1834. Impressed by the tribe's enthusiasm for summertime entertainment, he wrote, "The most beautiful was decidedly the ball-playing. . . . have sat, and almost dropped from my horse's back with irresistible laughter at the succession of droll tricks and kicks and scuffles which ensue in the almost superhuman struggles for the ball." Catlin watched a game of ishtaboli near Skullyville, which he painted and described in his book Letters and Notes on the Manners, Customs, and Conditions of the North American Indians:

A Game of Ishtaboli *(continued from page 9)*

Monday afternoon, at three o'clock, I rode out to a pretty prairie, the ball-playground of the Choctaws. . . . There were two points of timber about half a mile apart, in which the two parties for the play, with their respective families and friends were encamped.

All preparations were made by some old men who were selected to be the judges. They drew a line from one goal to the other. Immediately from the woods on both sides of the field a great concourse of women and old men, boys and girls, dogs and horses came up to the line drawn across the center of the field to place their bets. The betting was all done across this line. It seemed to be chiefly left to the women who martialled out a little of everything their houses and their fields contained: Goods and chattels, knives, dresses, blankets, pots and kettles, dogs and horses and guns. All were placed in the possession of stakeholders, who sat by them and watched them all night preparatory to the play.

This game had been arranged and "made up" three or four months before the parties met to play it, in the following manner: The two champions who led the two parties chose players alternately from the whole tribe. They each sent runners with ball-sticks, fantastically ornamented with ribbons and red paint, to be touched by each one of the chosen players, who thereby agreed to be on the spot at the appointed time and ready for the play.

Once the field was prepared, and preliminaries of the game all settled, the bettings all made and goods all "staked," night came on without the appearance of any players on the ground. But soon after dark, a procession of lighted flambeaux [torches] was seen coming from each encampment. The players assembled around their respective goals. At the beat of the drums and chants of the women, each party of players commenced the "ball-play dance." Each party danced for a quarter of an hour around their respective goals in their ball-play dress; rattling their ball-sticks together in the most violent manner, and all singing as loud as they could. Meanwhile, the women of each party, who had their goods at stake, formed into two rows on the line between the two parties of players, and also danced in a uniform step, all their voices joined in chants to the Great Spirit. In the meantime, four old medicine-men, who were to be the judges of the play, were seated at midfield. They were busily smoking to the Great Spirit, too, for their success in judging rightly between the parties in so important an affair.

The dance was repeated at intervals of every half hour all night. The players were certainly awake all night, but prepared for play the next morning.

In the morning, at the appointed hour, the game commenced with the judges throwing up the ball and firing a gun. An instant struggle ensued between the players, as some six or seven hundred men mutually endeavored to catch the ball in their sticks and throw it into their opponent's goal. Hundreds ran together and leapt over each other's heads, and darted between their adversaries' legs, tripping and throwing and foiling each other in every possible manner. Every voice was raised in shrill yelps and barks. There were rapid successions of feats, and of incidents.

Every trick is used that can be devised, to oppose the progress of the ball. These obstructions often meet desperate resistance, which terminate in a violent scuffle, and sometimes fisticuffs. Sticks are dropped, and the parties are unmolested as they settle it between themselves.

At times, when the ball is on the ground, such a confused mass rushes around it, and knocks their sticks together, there is no possibility of anyone seeing it. The condensed mass of ball-sticks, and shins, and bloody noses, travels around the different parts of the field for a quarter of an hour at a time. Since no one can see the ball, several minutes may pass while the mob struggles even though the ball is being played over another part of the field.

Each time the ball passes between the stakes of either party, one point is counted for game, and there is a halt of about one minute. Then play is started again by the judges. The struggle continues until the successful party gets to one hundred, which is the limit of the game. It was not finished until an hour before sunset. The winners take their stakes. Then, by previous agreement, a number of jugs of whisky were produced, which sent them all off merry and in good humor.

(continued from page 9)

followed complicated rules of play and etiquette, ishtaboli was a bruising and vicious game. Players often suffered broken bones when they were hit or tackled.

The Choctaws believed in spiritual entities, but they probably did not worship a single supreme being. However, they did consider the sun to be a particularly powerful force. The Choctaws also thought that some members of their society possessed special powers and they often consulted these enchanters, healers, rainmakers, and prophets. Their *alikchi*, or medicine men, used their powers to predict future events, to help hunters enjoy success in the chase, or to instill bravery in warriors. Some alikchi were skilled in treating wounds and diagnosing diseases and knew of many plants and other antidotes that could cure various illnesses. Other alikchi were known to call on supernatural forces for evil purposes.

The Choctaws believed that every person had two souls that survived after death. These souls were not purely spiritual but took the form of a *shilup*, a ghost in the shape of a human. Upon death, one shilup, the "outside shadow," remained in the Choctaw homeland to frighten the living. The other, the "inside shadow," went to one of two afterworlds. Both were located on earth, but were a great distance away. After death, most Choctaws traveled to the good afterworld, which was a pleasant, sunny land, with plenty of animals for good hunting. Tribespeople who had committed murder, however, went to the bad afterworld, a cloudy and rainy place, with few animals to hunt. Its inhabitants were destined to an eternity of misery and discomfort.

When a Choctaw died, the corpse was wrapped in animal skin or tree bark and placed on a scaffold five to six feet from the ground. Friends and relatives visited the scaffold to cry, mourn, and wail. When the body had decomposed, a painted and tattooed tribal official, known as a bone picker, would scrape off any remaining flesh from the bones with his long fingernails as the bereaved watched. The scaffold was then burned, and the bones were placed in a box, which was stored in a community bone house. Once the ceremony was over, the bone picker presided over a feast. Several times a year, when the bone house became full, the bones were removed and buried in a mound. A communal funeral was then performed, attended by everyone in the village.

Perhaps the most distinguishing trait of the prehistoric Choctaws was the tribe's peaceful demeanor. The Choctaws almost never initiated warfare against their Indian neighbors, although they vigorously defended themselves whenever their lands were invaded. The practicality and adaptability that helped the early Choctaws avoid conflict also allowed them to develop their well-ordered social and political systems and their thriving agricultural economy. These qualities would be severely tested, however, when Europeans first arrived in the land of the Choctaws in the mid-sixteenth century. Despite the tribe's inclination, the Choctaws were to learn that war with these invaders could not always be avoided and that the price of preventing conflict with them would always be great.

2

Europeans and Changing Ways

By late 1540, Choctaw district chief Tuscaloosa knew that Hernando de Soto was coming. More than a year earlier the Spanish explorer and his men had landed in North America near what is today Tampa Bay in Florida. Tuscaloosa had heard reports that the Spaniards were traveling northwest into the continent, pillaging entire villages along their way. They usually demanded food and other goods from the Indians they encountered and often enslaved Native people to work as servants and baggage carriers. Because the Spaniards seldom stayed in one location for any length of time, Tuscaloosa hoped to be able to extend hospitality to de Soto and his soldiers, meet their minimum requests, and then quickly see them on their way.

De Soto arrived in Tuscaloosa's village in the eastern portion of the Choctaw domain early in October 1540. The first meeting between the explorer and the chief was cordial. They ate together, and later the Choctaws performed a dance for the Spaniards. The following day de Soto demanded carriers, canoes, and women. Tuscaloosa gave de Soto some Choctaw carriers, built the Spaniards rafts (because the Choctaws had no canoes), and promised to supply the soldiers with women when the Europeans reached the Choctaw village of Mabila (near present-day Mobile, Alabama). Tuscaloosa secretly sent a message to the chief of Mabila, warning him of the approaching Spaniards and cautioning him to be prepared to defend his town should the need arise.

Forcing Tuscaloosa and several of his assistants to join them, the Spaniards soon departed for Mabila. When the party arrived there on October 18, 1540, it was greeted by the Choctaws with dances, songs, and chants. Tuscaloosa then presented de Soto with a gift. Reminding de Soto that his demands had been met, the chief then requested his own release. When de Soto hesitated, Tuscaloosa walked away, entered a dwelling that was surrounded by many Choctaws armed with bows and arrows, and refused to come out. Inspired by Tuscaloosa's act of defiance, the Choctaws then attacked de Soto and his men, driving the Spaniards out of the village. The Choctaws unchained the men who had been enslaved and seized the Spaniards' baggage, which the carriers had placed inside the palisade (village wall) before the battle began. Among the spoils were two hundred pounds of pearls, Christian sacramental vessels, food, wine, clothing, and some arms and ammunition.

Outside the palisade, de Soto and his men regrouped and prepared to attack Mabila. In the battle that followed, the Choctaws' bows and arrows, which could not penetrate the European soldiers' metal armor, proved no match for the Spaniards' firearms and lances. The Spaniards regained entry into the village and set the stockade and several houses on fire. Many Choctaws were killed in the bloody battle, and some died in the fire. Several of the Choctaws who survived hanged themselves from trees with their bowstrings rather than allow

Hernando de Soto (shown here arriving at the Mississippi River) first entered the eastern portion of Choctaw territory in October 1540. Though the Spaniards were initially cordial to the Choctaws, they quickly showed their duplicitous nature by setting fire to the town of Mabila (near present-day Mobile, Alabama) and killing some fifteen hundred men, women, and children.

themselves to become prisoners of the Spaniards. As many as fifteen hundred Choctaw men, women, and children, including Tuscaloosa, lost their lives. Spanish casualties were estimated at only 22 dead and 148 wounded.

De Soto remained in Mabila until his wounded men had healed and his soldiers had seized enough corn and other supplies to continue their journey. On November 14, 1540, de Soto and more than five hundred men finally left the village. They headed northwest and eventually crossed from the eastern portion of the Choctaw homeland into the land of the Chickasaw Indians, where they became the first Europeans to see the Mississippi River.

Following the departure of de Soto, the Choctaws did not have any sustained contact with Europeans for one hundred fifty years, although foreign explorers and settlers continued to travel to North America. The Spanish claimed vast areas of land in present-day Florida, Mexico, and the western United States; the English built colonies along the Atlantic Coast; and the French explored much of Canada and the Mississippi River valley. But because very few of these Europeans came to live on the Choctaws' lands, the tribe continued to live for the next century and a half in much the same way it had before its first disastrous encounter with whites.

Not until the beginning of the eighteenth century did Europeans start to exert an influence over the Indians in what is now the southeastern United States. The Spanish had the least authority in the area because of the small population of their settlements; although Spanish missionaries and traders in Pensacola (in present-day northwestern Florida) had contact with the neighboring Indian tribes. English settlers, especially those in the highly populated colony of Carolina (now portions of North Carolina, South Carolina, and Georgia), had much more interaction with inland Indians. Trade with these tribes was one of their primary economic activities.

The French had become the dominant European presence in the lower Mississippi Valley and, therefore, they were to have the greatest influence on the Choctaws. In the late seventeenth century, Louis Jolliet and Jacques Marquette, and later René-Robert Cavelier, Sieur de La Salle, had explored much of the Mississippi River. Under the leadership of Pierre Le Moyne, Sieur d'Iberville, the French established a permanent settlement at Fort Maurepas, on the coast of the Gulf of Mexico near old Biloxi (now Ocean Springs), in 1699. More French settlements soon followed: Mobile, located on the Gulf Coast, in 1702; Fort Rosalie, at Natchez on the Mississippi River, in 1716; New Orleans, at the mouth of the river, in 1718; and Fort St. Pierre, at Yazoo, north of Natchez on the Yazoo River, in 1719.

As more and more Europeans came to North America, competition among England, Spain, and France for dominance on the continent increased. So did the nations' desire for military and trade alliances with the Indians. The English in particular relied on trade with the Indians, because slaves had become vital to the economy of the English colonies. The colonists imported African slaves to work as field hands, carpenters, blacksmiths, and mechanics, but they also traded guns, ammunition, knives, axes, hoes, and cooking utensils to some Indians in exchange for Indian slaves whom they captured from other tribes. There were many Indian slaves in Carolina, but others were sent to New England or the West Indies. In addition to trade, it was important for all three powers—England, Spain, and France—to gain Indian military support in order to strengthen their own position and guard their claims on the continent against their European rivals. Therefore, much of the history of the eighteenth century in North America involves the conflict between European settlers and their struggle for power and to gain an advantage over one another. For the Indians, this struggle often meant almost continual warfare, because each European power encouraged its Indian allies to battle its European rivals and their respective Indian allies.

With the French to their west and the English to their east, the Choctaws held a strategic position that led both colonial powers to seek their allegiance. The tribe almost always preferred the French; initially because the French presence on the Mississippi River made them the most available trading partners and also because the French governors had given gifts to the Choctaw chiefs from the start of their contact. The Choctaws, however, soon came to see the English as enemies after the English-allied Chickasaw Indians to the north began to raid Choctaw villages as well as those of neighboring tribes, such as the Taena and the Tunica, and took Indian slaves. The Choctaws and the Chickasaws had been warring for several years when Choctaw leaders met with the French at old Biloxi in 1699 to discuss their mutual dislike of the English. Seeing an opportunity to hurt their European rival, the French agreed to aid the Choctaws in their battles against the English and the Chickasaws.

The Choctaw-Chickasaw conflict continued until French colonial leader d'Iberville invited representatives of several area tribes to meet with him at a council in Mobile in 1702. D'Iberville persuaded the Chickasaws to become the allies of the French and the Choctaws. This peace lasted less than two years. Enraged that the Chickasaws had resumed their trading relations with the English, again providing them with goods and slaves, the Choctaws attacked the Chickasaws in 1703, and the war between the tribes resumed. Another peace agreement was made in 1708, but fighting began again in 1711, when the Creeks and Chickasaws, with English backing, invaded the Choctaw homeland and inflicted heavy casualties. After this successful campaign by the English, the Choctaws became allies of England. Not surprisingly, this shift in allegiance was short-lived. By 1715, the Choctaws were back with the French, and by 1720, the French and Choctaws were once again at war with the Chickasaws, in a conflict that lasted for the next five years.

By the end of the 1720s, the French were also at war with the Natchez Indians, who lived along the Mississippi River near present-day Natchez, Mississippi. Relations between the French and the Natchez had once been good, but the Natchez became hostile as French settlers began to take control of more and more of their fertile land on the river. Possibly encouraged by the Chickasaws and the English, the tribe began a series of attacks on French settlements. The most violent of these occurred in 1729, when the Natchez stormed Fort Rosalie, which the Indians themselves had built for the French thirteen years earlier. The Natchez slaughtered two hundred fifty soldiers, took nearly three hundred women and children prisoner, and almost destroyed the fort. With the aid of the Choctaws, the enraged French struck back in 1730 and rescued their prisoners. By 1731, they had practically annihilated the entire Natchez tribe. The survivors came to live with the Chickasaws and the Cherokees or were captured and sold into slavery, usually in the West Indies.

After nearly fifty years of constant warfare and shifting allegiances, the Choctaws began to fight among themselves. Okla Falaya had become sympathetic to the English, Okla Tannap remained loyal to the French, and Okla Hannali was divided. The two factions grew so unfriendly that a civil war broke out within the tribe in 1748, resulting in heavy losses to both sides. Soon, French leader Carlos de Grandpré intervened and with a detachment of French soldiers, helped defeat the pro-English Choctaw faction. In 1750, peace was established through the Grandpré Treaty, in which the French imposed some harsh controls on the Choctaw people. The *treaty* stated that any Choctaw who killed a Frenchman or invited an Englishman to a Choctaw village would be put to death. It also provided that the Choctaws would continue to battle the Chickasaws and "never cease to strike at that perfidious race as long as there should be any portion of it remaining."

The Grandpré Treaty helped fuel the Choctaws' growing disillusionment with their French allies. In 1754, angry because the French had stopped their regular distribution of gifts to the tribe, the Choctaws threatened to enter into an allegiance with the English. Their demands received little attention, however, because the French were occupied with battling the English in the French and Indian War, which had erupted to the east in the same year. This final war between France and England for supremacy in North America ended in 1763 with the signing of the Treaty of Paris. England agreed to return Cuba to Spain in exchange for the territory of Florida. The defeated French ceded Canada to the English, gave their lands west of the river (known as Louisiana) to the Spanish, and relinquished all claims to other territory east of the Mississippi River. Thus, French colonial ambitions in North America came to an end.

The English attempted to establish control over the territory between their settlements along the Atlantic Coast and the Mississippi River by making treaties with various inland Indian groups, including the Choctaws, Chickasaws, Cherokees, and Creeks. In 1765, the Choctaws met with British authorities in Mobile, where they signed a treaty that defined their eastern boundary approximately at the Alabama and Cahaba Rivers in Alabama and prohibited English settlers from moving into their land. While encamped there, the Choctaws were attacked by the Creek Indians, which led to a war that lasted for six years. Fearing the belligerent Creeks, the English encouraged the Chickasaws and Cherokees to join the fighting on the side of the Choctaws.

The Choctaws' loyalties to the English were not strong, however. During the American Revolution (1775–1783), some Choctaws served as scouts for the American armies as they battled British troops. The Americans emerged victorious, and as part of the terms of the 1783 Treaty of Paris, England surrendered its North American territory east of the Mississippi River and south of Canada to the United States, with the exception of East and West Florida, which it granted to Spain. The Choctaws were not disappointed that their land was no longer under British control.

Nearly eighty years of contact with the English and the French had left their mark on the Choctaws, however. The intermarriage of Europeans and Choctaws particularly disrupted the tribe's traditional society by reducing the influence of the clan system and tribal customs. The increasing number of Choctaws of mixed ancestry also made it easier for the tribe to accept the values of non-Indian society.

Even more disturbing to the traditional Choctaw way of life were the consequences of the continual wars the tribe had waged at the insistence of its European allies. Before contact with Europeans, the Choctaws had been a nonaggressive people, with no desire to expand their territory. But their allegiances, particularly with the French, led the Choctaws knowingly, although possibly unwillingly at times, to aid their European allies' attempts to extend their influence on the American continent. As a result, the Choctaws had been at war for most of the eighteenth century, battling among themselves as well as against neighboring tribes and colonial intruders. The few new European trade goods and diplomatic skills the Choctaws had acquired were a small consolation for the constant conflict and loss of Choctaw lives. Now, under the control of the United States, the Choctaws would enter a period of increased contact with non-Indians, which would change their lives even more.

3

The Loss of the Homeland

Immediately after the end of the American Revolution, the United States set out to gain dominance over the vast amount of land it had acquired from England under the terms of the Treaty of Paris. Because there were few American settlers in the southwestern portion of this territory, the United States was particularly concerned about gaining support from the many Indians in the South and reducing the possibility of hostilities with Native tribes. To strengthen its influence, the U.S. government began to enter into a series of treaties with the southern Indians.

On January 3, 1786, the Choctaws signed the Treaty of Hopewell, the first of nine agreements they would make with the U.S. government between 1786 and 1830. The treaty established perpetual peace and friendship between the two parties, defined the eastern boundary of the Choctaws' territory as the same border described in the tribe's 1756 treaty with the English, gave the United States the right to build trading posts on Choctaw land, guaranteed the tribe would be protected by the U.S. Army, and provided that any U.S. citizen living within the territory of the Choctaws was subject to tribal jurisdiction.

The Spanish were concerned about the Choctaws' friendly relationship with the new U.S. government. They feared that American settlers would soon move westward into the Choctaw domain and, from there, eventually migrate into Spanish-owned lands west of the Mississippi River. To protect their interests, the Spanish established forts on the western and eastern borders of Choctaw land. They first purchased a tract of land from the Choctaws and Chickasaws on the western edge of Choctaw territory and built Fort Nogales near the mouth of the Yazoo River. There, the Spanish signed a treaty of friendship with the Choctaw, Chickasaw, Cherokee, and Creek tribes in 1792. The Spanish also convinced the Choctaws to sell another tract in the eastern section of their country near the Tombigbee River. The tribe was hesitant to part with this land, but the Spanish convinced the Indians that a Spanish fort at this location could protect them if the United States ever grew hostile. On this site, the Spanish constructed Fort Confederation.

The Spanish presence among the Choctaws did not last long. After the pro-Spanish Creeks were defeated in a series of clashes with the U.S.-supplied Chickasaws, the United States and Spain signed the Treaty of San Lorenzo (also called Pinckney's Treaty, after U.S. Major General Thomas Pinckney, who helped negotiate it in 1795). In the treaty, Spain agreed to remove its settlers from land north of the 31st parallel and was therefore forced to abandon Fort Nogales and Fort Confederation.

With the Spanish gone from the area, the United States was now able to set up a program for dealing with the Choctaws and other southern tribes. The government soon began to send *agents* to work with the different Indian groups. These officials were responsible for enforcing federal laws within the tribal domains. Also at this time, the U.S. government began to politically

In 1795, Major General Thomas Pinckney, the U.S. envoy to Spain, helped negotiate the treaty of San Lorenzo, which expanded the new nation's borders to the 31st parallel in southern Alabama and Mississippi to the south and the Mississippi River to the west. Though the treaty did not directly involve the Choctaws, it laid the groundwork for the United States to partition their land through a series of one-sided treaties that eventually forced the majority of Choctaws to move west.

organize the Indian country between the Mississippi River and the states located on the East Coast, anticipating that many white settlers would soon move west. In 1798, Mississippi Territory was formed from the southern portions of what are now Mississippi and Alabama. (The northern portions and the southern tips of these present-day states were added to Mississippi Territory in 1804 and 1812, respectively.)

The United States entered into its next two treaties with the Choctaws in order to buy portions of the tribe's territory for white settlers. With the Treaty of Fort Adams, signed on December 17, 1801, the U.S. government secured 2,264,920 acres of land in the southwest corner of the Choctaws' territory. It also gained the right to construct a road from the town of Natchez, on the Mississippi River, northeast across Choctaw country to Nashville, Tennessee. The Choctaws were compensated for the land with $2,000 in money and merchandise. The tribe was in desperate need of this payment because it was experiencing a famine as a result of a drought that had nearly destroyed its crops the year before the signing of the treaty. The United States also provided three sets of blacksmith's tools for the Choctaws whose homes were located in the ceded land.

On October 7, 1802, the Choctaws signed the Treaty of Fort Confederation. This agreement redefined the Choctaws' eastern boundary, resulting in the tribe's cession of about fifty thousand acres of land north of Mobile. Although the treaty granted the Choctaws only one dollar in compensation, the tribe was willing to give up this relatively small tract of hunting land in order to preserve its friendly relationship with the U.S. government.

After these cessions, many Americans quickly settled around Natchez, on the Mississippi, and north of Mobile, in the lower Tombigbee River valley. To accommodate this influx of American settlers, President Thomas Jefferson assigned General James Wilkinson to discuss yet another land cession with the Choctaw chiefs. General Wilkinson and the chiefs met at Hoe Buckintoopa, an Indian village near Mobile. The Choctaws initially refused to negotiate, but Wilkinson reminded the chiefs of debts the tribe owed to the British trading company of Panton, Leslie and Company, which was requesting immediate payment. The Choctaws reluctantly agreed to cede 853,760 acres of land north of Mobile if the U.S. government would pay their bill. The Choctaws and the United States signed the Treaty of Hoe Buckintoopa on August 31, 1803. In the agreement, the government compensated the chiefs by giving them each "15 pieces of stroud [woolen cloth], 3 rifles, 150 blankets, 250 rounds of powder, 250 pounds of lead, 1 bridle, 1 man's saddle, and 1 black silk handkerchief."

The liquidation of Choctaw debts in exchange for land was a ploy the U.S. government would use again in treaty negotiations with the Choctaws. In the Treaty of Mount Dexter (sometimes referred to as the First Choctaw Cession), signed on November 16, 1805, the Choctaws gave up 4,142,720 acres across the southern portion of Choctaw territory. The Choctaws did not want to sign the treaty, but the government induced them to do so by offering to pay back another debt the tribe owed to Panton, Leslie and Company, this one amounting to $48,000. The U.S. government also agreed to give the tribe an *annuity* (annual payment) of $3,000, which the chiefs would be allowed to spend in any way they saw fit. In addition, each of the district chiefs was given a cash payment of $500 and a salary of $150 a year while he remained in his office. The treaty marked the beginning of the United States' payment of annuities to the Choctaws, which established a permanent tribal income and continued the custom of giving gifts to the chiefs in exchange for their cooperation.

During the years in which the United States negotiated these treaties with the Choctaws, Spain lost control of much of its land in North America. Although Spain did not officially cede Florida to the United States until 1819, it had progressively less authority over the region as more and more American settlers moved into the area throughout the early 1800s. A more substantial loss was Louisiana, which Spain returned to France in 1800 because there were too few Spaniards living in this vast territory to protect it from encroachment by other European settlers.

In 1803, the United States bought Louisiana from France, a purchase that almost doubled the young country's area and moved its western border from the Mississippi River to the base of the Rocky Mountains. President Jefferson was eager to use this land as a place to relocate (remove) Indians living east of the Mississippi and thereby open up more territory in the eastern United States for non-Indian settlers. Although several years passed before the U.S. government put this *removal policy* into action, Congress passed the Louisiana Territorial Act in 1804, giving the president the power to negotiate with Indian tribes for their removal.

The threat of removal and the continuing movement of Americans into lands inhabited by Indians inspired Tecumseh, leader of the Shawnee Indians, to attempt to form an Indian confederacy. In 1811, Tecumseh and thirty warriors traveled south into Choctaw territory to elicit the tribe's support. After Tecumseh urged the Choctaws' council to rise up against white intruders, Choctaw Chief Pushmataha eloquently reminded his people of their long friendship with the United States. The council expelled Tecumseh, who then journeyed east into the land of the Creeks, whom he found much more receptive to his message. In August 1813, a band of Creek Indians massacred the white inhabitants of Fort Mims in Alabama Territory; an attack that sparked a long war between that tribe and the United States. Hundreds of Choctaw and Chickasaw warriors fought on the side of the U.S. Army in this conflict. Many had already demonstrated their loyalty to the United States by fighting alongside American soldiers against the British during the War of 1812.

The Creek War created boundary disputes that the Choctaw chiefs and U.S. government officials met to settle in 1816 at the trading post at St. Stephens on the Tombigbee River (a tributary of the Mobile River in western Alabama). In the Treaty of Fort St. Stephens (also called the Treaty of 1816), signed on October 24, the Choctaws ceded approximately three million acres of land east of the Tombigbee. The Choctaws were compensated with $10,000 in merchandise and a $6,000 annuity to be paid for twenty years. The parties agreed that the

U.S. government would bank the annual payment but would give the Choctaws the earned interest to establish and maintain Choctaw schools. The annual interest payment helped pay for the establishment of the first school in Choctaw territory, which was founded in 1818 at Elliot (near present-day Grenada, Mississippi). Cyrus Kingsbury, a Presbyterian missionary and former Cherokee school instructor, set up the institution at the Choctaws' invitation.

In 1817, the western portion of Mississippi Territory became the state of Mississippi, and, in 1819, the eastern portion became Alabama. This encouraged more and more whites to settle on the lands the Choctaws had ceded to the U.S. government. The population of the entire Mississippi Territory in 1800 was 8,850, but by 1820, the population of the state of Mississippi alone had grown to 75,448. Although the government tried to keep the newly arrived settlers and Indians at peace; as the number of settlers increased, so did the pressure they exerted on the United States to obtain more land from the Indians and to remove entire tribes to territory farther west.

The United States tried to acquire additional Choctaw land in 1818 and 1819, but the tribe refused to cede any more territory. Finally, in October 1820, Generals Andrew Jackson and Thomas Hinds and Choctaw Chiefs Pushmataha, Moshulatubbee, and Apukshunnubbee met at Doak's Stand, a grassy flat near the Pearl River in central Mississippi. After much discussion and argument, the Choctaws reluctantly signed the Treaty of Doak's Stand on October 18, 1820. Through this agreement, the Choctaws gave up 5,169,788 acres of their domain in exchange for approximately 13 million acres of land to the west. Most of the new land was in present-day Oklahoma and western Arkansas, between the Red River to the south and the Arkansas and Canadian Rivers to the north—territory the U.S. government had acquired from the Quapaw Indians in 1818. In the treaty, Jackson also arranged for every Choctaw man to receive "a blanket, kettle, rifle gun, bullet molds and wipers, and ammunition sufficient for hunting and defense for one year plus enough corn . . . for one year."

After the treaty was signed, the United States expected the Choctaws to emigrate. The Choctaws' new land, however, had not been fully surveyed, and its exact boundaries were not known. When the area was finally surveyed, the United States discovered that many white settlers were already living on the land owned by the Choctaws in what is now western Arkansas. The U.S. government decided that a new treaty should be drawn up.

The Choctaws sent a delegation to Washington, D.C., in the late fall of 1824 to speak with representatives of the federal government about the problems stemming from the Treaty of Doak's Stand. Upon their arrival, the Choctaws were wined and dined by U.S. officials, who believed negotiations would be easier if the Choctaw leaders were intoxicated by "firewater." The government's bar bill for the conference amounted to a staggering $2,149.50, with an additional $2,029 spent on food and lodgings for the Choctaws. Each delegate was also given a suit of clothes at a total cost of $1,134.74.

Tragedy struck the delegation when Chief Pushmataha died from pneumonia in Washington on Christmas Eve. Chief Apukshunnubbee had been killed en route to Washington as a result of a fall from a cliff. Chief Moshulatubbee, therefore, was the only district chief left in the delegation when the negotiations were concluded.

On January 20, 1825, Chief Moshulatubbee and Secretary of War John Calhoun signed the Treaty of 1825 (also called the Treaty of Washington City). The treaty redefined the eastern boundary of the Choctaw land in the newly designated *Indian Territory* (present-day Oklahoma) as a line extending from the Arkansas River near Fort Smith due south to the Red River, which is approximately the boundary between Arkansas and Oklahoma today. The Choctaws had ceded about two million acres of the land given to them at Doak's

Stand, but, in return, the U.S. government agreed to move all white settlers living to the west of the new boundary out of the Choctaws' territory and not to permit any more whites to cross this border. In addition, the Choctaws received a perpetual annuity of $6,000, a waiver of back debts they owed to trading companies, and pensions for all Choctaw veterans who fought in the War of 1812.

The United States now hoped the Choctaws would voluntarily remove to Indian Territory. A few did in the late 1820s, and by 1829, a small settlement, later known as Skullyville, was established near Fort Smith, Arkansas. But this gradual emigration was too slow to suit the white settlers in Mississippi. In 1829, the Mississippi state legislature extended its laws over the Choctaws, and in January 1830, the Choctaws were granted Mississippi state citizenship, and their tribal government was abolished. When Choctaw leaders then began to challenge the pressures put on them by the U.S. and Mississippi governments, the United States decided that another treaty was needed to induce the Choctaws to remove to Indian Territory and to secure the more than ten million acres of land the tribe still retained in Mississippi and Alabama.

President Andrew Jackson sent Secretary of State John H. Eaton and Colonel John Coffee to negotiate the treaty in September 1830. Choctaw leaders Greenwood LeFlore, Moshulatubbee, and Nitakechi, and approximately six thousand Choctaws met the government representatives between the two prongs of Dancing Rabbit Creek in present-day Noxubee County in eastern Mississippi. The meeting officially opened on September 18 in a festive atmosphere. During the day, Eaton and Coffee made speeches, which John Pitchlynn, a white man who had long lived among the Choctaws, interpreted for the tribe. In the evening, many Choctaws danced and visited the saloons and gambling tables that had been set up inside tents on the treaty-negotiation grounds. U.S. officials did not permit missionaries and the converted Choctaws to camp on the grounds because they feared the Christian Indians would object to the consumption of alcohol and interfere with the negotiations.

Over the next few days, Choctaw leaders discussed the details of the proposed treaty with Eaton and Coffee. During their meetings, as many as sixty councilmen would sit in a circle, with a small number of selected older Choctaw women seated in the center. Although the women did not participate actively in the discussions, they made their feelings known to the councilmen before and after the meetings.

On Wednesday, September 22, the Choctaws voted on whether to accept the treaty. Only one Choctaw leader, Killihota, favored removal. When the Choctaws voted the next day against removal a second time, Secretary Eaton became irate. He threatened that if the Choctaws refused to sign the treaty, the president would declare war against the tribe and send U.S. troops into Choctaw territory. By Friday, September 24, negotiations had broken down, and many Choctaws left the treaty grounds. Sensing that those who remained were inclined toward removal, Eaton and Coffee asked Greenwood LeFlore to help them draft another treaty. They knew that LeFlore, the chief of the Upper Towns District (formerly known as Okla Falaya), was a supporter of removal and had a strong following among the mixed-blood members of the tribe. Talks continued over the next several days about the specific provisions of the treaty while Eaton coerced and intimidated the Choctaws.

Finally, on Monday, September 27, 1830, Choctaw leaders, led by LeFlore and Moshulatubbee, signed the Treaty of Dancing Rabbit Creek. In it, the Choctaws ceded their remaining land in Mississippi and agreed to move to Indian Territory. In return, the United States promised to protect the Choctaws in their new homeland and guaranteed the tribe an annuity of $20,000 for twenty years, along with additional money to build schools, churches, and a council house there. However, the treaty's

Moshulatubbee, whose name means "Warrior Who Perseveres," was one of three Choctaw chiefs who signed the Treaty of Dancing Rabbit Creek on September 27, 1830, which called for the removal of the Choctaws from Mississippi to present-day southeastern Oklahoma. From 1834 until Oklahoma became a state in 1907, the area between the Arkansas River and the Winding Star Mountains in the Choctaw Nation was known as the Moshulatubbee District.

Article 14, a contribution made by LeFlore, gave the Choctaws an opportunity to remain in Mississippi. It stated that a Choctaw family could elect to stay and become citizens of the United States as long as the family head registered this intention with the Choctaw agent in Mississippi within six months.

The head of the family would then receive 640 acres of land, plus an additional 320 acres for each child over ten years of age living with the family and 160 acres for each child under the age of ten. With the signing of this treaty, the story of two separate groups of Choctaws—one in Indian Territory and one in Mississippi—would begin. (For additional information on the treaty of Dancing Rabbit Creek, as well as other Choctaw treaties with the U.S. government, enter "Choctaw treaties" into any search engine and browse the many sites listed.)

While the Choctaw chiefs and the U.S. government negotiated the treaties that ultimately resulted in the tribe's division and loss of its homeland, the daily life of the average Choctaw was undergoing tremendous social and cultural changes— the greatest of which occurred in 1818 with the arrival of missionaries. Like the U.S. government, missionaries attempted to "civilize" the Indians by teaching them the values of non-Indian society. Although the Choctaws, at least initially, did not embrace Christianity, they enthusiastically supported the schools that Christian missionaries founded in their domain. For instance, Elliot, the first Choctaw school, was initially funded by the Presbyterian mission board, but the Choctaws soon offered the instructors the $200 annual interest payment they received from the federal government under the terms of the Treaty of Fort St. Stephens. The Choctaw people also donated $500 a year, and by 1820, the Choctaw council had agreed to pay $6,000 annually for seventeen years to support the school. Shortly after Elliot was established in 1818, Methodist and Baptist missionaries came to practice among the Choctaws. By 1825, thirteen mission schools were operating in Choctaw country.

In these schools, the missionaries taught many Choctaw children to read and write in the Choctaw language with the Roman alphabet, the same alphabet used to write in English. They also introduced the Choctaws to agricultural innovations, animal husbandry, and homemaking. During this time, the

Choctaws began to grow cotton, which students were taught to spin and weave into clothing. As the tribe became more educated, its economy came to rely less on hunting and more on industry and agriculture.

The Choctaws adopted the new ways readily, in part because of the increasing influence and number of tribespeople of mixed Indian and white heritage. Several so-called mixed-bloods had become leaders in the tribe in the 1820s. The sons of Indian women and white men who had settled in Choctaw country in the late eighteenth century, Greenwood LeFlore, Peter Pitchlynn, and David Folsom were particularly well regarded within the tribe.

As the tribe's contact with white settlers increased, certain traditional Choctaw customs began to change. Because Christian missionaries condemned the practices of the Choctaws' traditional medicine men, some Choctaws stopped consulting their tribal healers. The tribe's distinctive burial practices were abandoned as well. They ceased to place their dead on scaffolds and no longer employed a bone picker. The Choctaws now buried their corpses in a sitting position surrounded by the deceased's personal possessions. The family would go to the grave to weep and cry; and at the end of the mourning period, a ceremony and a feast were held.

The Choctaws' system of justice also underwent a transformation. Traditionally, if a Choctaw committed a crime, he or she would be punished by the victim's relatives. If the accused could not be found, a member of his or her family was substituted; however, most violators voluntarily submitted to punishment. But now, a Choctaw charged with a criminal offense was subject instead to a trial by a jury of light horsemen, the mounted patrols the Choctaws established to dispense justice. A band of light horsemen would travel through each district, serving as sheriffs as well as judges. For minor offenses, a criminal was lashed; for major offenses such as murder, the person was shot.

Despite these adaptations, the Choctaws retained much of their traditional way of life. They were still primarily agriculturalists, growing corn, beans, squash, and other crops; but they also continued to fish, hunt, and gather fruits and nuts to supplement the food supply; and they performed the same dances and played the same games the tribe had enjoyed for centuries. For the three hundred years following the Choctaws' first contact with Europeans, the tribe had struggled to learn how to coexist with whites by adopting elements of their society, while also maintaining its traditional Indian customs. Removal now presented the Choctaws with the new challenge of reconstructing this hybrid *culture* in an unfamiliar area hundreds of miles from their homeland.

4

Struggle and Prosperity

A s soon as the Treaty of Dancing Rabbit Creek was signed in 1830, some Choctaws migrated to Indian Territory, hoping to claim the best land there. The majority of the Choctaws, however, waited to be removed in three successive journeys that the U.S. government scheduled for 1831, 1832, and 1833. The *Bureau of Indian Affairs* (BIA), the government office formed by the War Department in 1824 to manage Native American affairs, planned to relocate each year about one-third of the Choctaw population, which at the time numbered between eighteen and twenty thousand.

Anticipating the difficulty of transporting entire eastern tribes to distant Indian Territory, the BIA had chosen to remove the Choctaws first because of the tribe's long history of cooperation with the U.S. government. Secretary of War John Eaton gave the responsibility for preparing the removal to agent George S. Gaines, whom the Choctaws knew and trusted. Gaines was dedicated to making the ordeal as easy

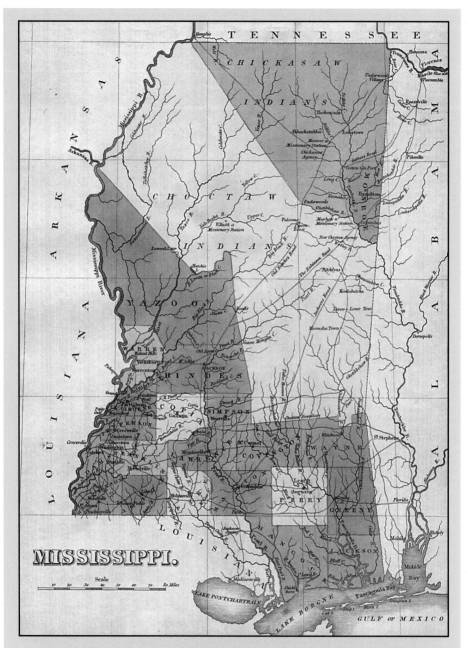

A map of Mississippi, c. 1826, four years prior to the Treaty of Dancing Rabbit Creek, when the Choctaws ceded their remaining land in the state to the U.S. government. The Choctaws' territory originally encompassed much of Mississippi and western Alabama, but by 1826, was confined to the central part of Mississippi.

on the tribe as possible, but the enormous task of organizing this 550-mile trek through unsettled country proved extremely complicated. The plans became especially muddled after Lewis Cass, who replaced Eaton as secretary of war in April 1831, dismissed many of the officials Gaines had hired to help with the removal.

In the late fall of 1831, the first group of Choctaws made their way to Memphis and Vicksburg, two cities on the Mississippi River that served as departure points. Gaines had secured five steamboats—the *Walter Scott*, the *Brandywine*, the *Reindeer*, the *Talma*, and the *Cleopatra*—that transported the Choctaws up the Mississippi River to various tributaries, namely, the Ouachita, Arkansas, and White Rivers. Other steamboats took the Indians northwest up these rivers as far as the boats could travel without being grounded in shallow water. The Choctaws then walked to Indian Territory from towns such as Ecore à Fabre, Washington, Little Rock, and Rockroe. Upon their arrival, many Choctaws registered at Fort Towson, Mountain Fork, Old Miller Court House, and Horse Prairie, near the Red River in the southeastern corner of their new land. Others went to the Choctaw Agency near the Arkansas River in the northeastern section.

For this first party of Choctaws, removal was a bitter experience. The southern Mississippi Valley was hit by one of the worst snowstorms in its history in the winter of 1831. Because the BIA had not purchased enough provisions and equipment for the journey, few of the Choctaws had blankets, shoes, or winter clothing, and many died in the zero-degree weather. Heavy rains also washed out some roads and trails, which made their travel much slower. Able to cover only fifteen miles a day, the Choctaws soon depleted their already inadequate food supply, and hundreds starved to death. (For additional information on this forced emigration, enter "Choctaw Trail of Tears" into any search engine and browse the many sites listed.)

Morale among the Choctaws remaining in Mississippi was low after they heard reports of the first removal. Nevertheless, about six thousand to seven thousand agreed to emigrate in the second group, which departed in October 1832. Although the journey began well, icy winds and rain again slowed travel, and many in the party became infected with cholera, a gastrointestinal disease that proved fatal in most cases. Because the cost of the first removal had been twice what the BIA had anticipated, Cass had fired Gaines and put the U.S. Army in charge of preparing the next two removal expeditions. To economize, the army had reduced the food rations for each Choctaw and ordered only five small wagons for every thousand Indians, so that even the elderly and infirm had to walk the last leg of their journey. William Armstrong, an army captain who assisted in the second removal, observed, "Fortunately, they are a people that will walk to the last, or I do not know how we could go on." News of these horrors discouraged most of the Choctaws still in Mississippi from joining the third removal party in December 1833. Although good weather made this journey much easier than the previous two, there were only nine hundred Choctaws in this group. After they arrived in Indian Territory in the spring of 1834, the Choctaw population there was approximately 11,500. A total of about 14,000 Choctaws had left Mississippi in the three removal parties, but at least 2,500 had died on the trip west.

The Choctaws who remained in their homeland, however, did not fare much better than those who had been removed. According to Article 14 of the Treaty of Dancing Rabbit Creek, every Choctaw family that elected to stay in Mississippi had to register with the Choctaw Agency within six months in order to be eligible for land ownership. But Colonel William Ward, the U.S. agent for the Mississippi Choctaws at the time, refused to let some of the Indians register. Ward lost or misplaced the records of many of those he did register, and, in some cases, he simply removed names from his lists. Ward was particularly hesitant to register full-blooded Choctaws, because he hoped that they would choose to remove to Indian Territory rather than remain behind. Although the Bureau of Indian Affairs did not condone Colonel Ward's actions, it did little to curtail them. While John Eaton was secretary of war, he had even dispatched a cavalry unit to Mississippi to see that the Choctaws—particularly those who were full-blooded—were encouraged to emigrate. Many Indians turned to the state government of Mississippi for help and protection, but the state, which was busy selling the ceded Choctaw homeland to land speculators and white settlers, offered little assistance. Although Colonel Ward was finally dismissed by the U.S. government in 1833, allegedly because there were not enough Indians left in Mississippi to justify an agent, only sixty-nine heads of Choctaw families—thirty full-bloods and thirty-nine mixed-bloods—were ever officially registered. The vast majority of the approximately six thousand Choctaws who remained in Mississippi, therefore, never received the land to which they were entitled.

Life for the Mississippi Choctaws was difficult throughout the 1830s. Many suffered from poverty and hunger, and their standard of living was described by observers at the time as lower than that of the black slaves in the state. Because most of the missionaries among the Choctaws had removed with the majority of the tribe, these Indians no longer had access to schools or churches. Whites continually harassed them, often fining or imprisoning them for minor infractions or burning their houses and tearing down their fences. Most of the Mississippi Choctaws became *squatters*, landless settlers who lived in isolated areas on poor farmland to which they had no legal title. To survive, they gathered wild berries and nuts and planted corn, pumpkins, and potatoes, and some raised chickens and hogs. A few worked on nearby farms of white settlers, earning fifty cents a day for picking and hoeing cotton. But despite their situation, these dispossessed Choctaws retained their tribal identity. They were still bonded by language and custom, even though they no longer had any common land or government.

Once the Choctaws in Indian Territory had recovered from the trauma of removal, their experience was much different from that of their Mississippi kin. In possession of a vast expanse of land and a regular annuity income, they were immediately able to begin to rebuild the culture they had known in Mississippi. First, they established settlements close to the eastern border of their territory in three districts, which they named after the chiefs who had negotiated the Treaty of Doak's Stand. Pushmataha, to the west of the Kiamichi River, was settled by Chief Nitakechi's followers; Apukshunnubbee, to the east of the Kiamichi, was founded by Chief LeFlore's people; and Moshulatubbee, north of the other two districts and south of the Arkansas and Canadian Rivers, was established by the followers of Chief Moshulatubbee. Moshulatubbee and Nitakechi led their people to these areas, but Greenwood LeFlore had decided to stay in Mississippi despite his earlier support for the tribe's removal. His nephew George W. Harkins and later his cousin Thomas LeFlore succeeded him as chief.

The Choctaws wasted no time in developing their new land. They soon began to farm along the floodplains of the Arkansas, Red, and Kiamichi Rivers and to raise cattle, sheep, and horses in the hillier regions of their territory. In the fall of 1833, only months after the second removal, the Choctaws had already produced a surplus of forty thousand bushels of corn, which they sold to the U.S. government to aid future Choctaw immigrants. Within a few years, the Choctaws were also raising potatoes, peas, beans, oats, rye, wheat, pumpkins, and melons. Cotton was also grown on large plantations along the Red River. These large farms were cultivated with the help of black slaves a few Choctaw slave owners had brought from Mississippi.

The Choctaws soon established several small but prosperous towns along trails that were traveled by easterners migrating

Chief George W. Harkins is best known for the open letter he addressed to the American people in which he denounced the policy of removal that had been adopted by the U.S. government after the Indian Removal Act was passed by Congress in 1830. In the letter, Harkins made it clear that the Choctaws were forced to leave their ancestral lands and would rather "suffer and be free, than live under the degrading influence of law."

to Texas or California. Among the earliest were Skullyville and Perryville in Moshulatubbee, Doaksville and Eagletown in Apukshunnubbee, and Boggy Depot in Pushmataha. Boggy Depot's location at the junction of two trails made it a major trading center, and Doaksville eventually became the largest town in Indian Territory.

The Choctaws held their first tribal council meeting in Indian Territory at Jack's Fork, at the center of the three districts, in 1834. There, on June 3, the tribe adopted a new constitution to govern the Choctaw Nation. Written in both Choctaw and English, it provided that all national business would be transacted by a general council composed of the three chiefs and twenty-seven councilmen, nine from each district. Only this general council would have the power to pass a law, which would have to be supported by two-thirds of the council members before it could be put into effect. In 1837, the Choctaws erected a large log council house at Jack's Fork. They named the building Nanih Waiya after the sacred mound in the Choctaws' Mississippi homeland.

As quickly as possible, the tribal government set about forming a new Choctaw school system. The missionaries who had removed with the tribe established mission schools soon after they arrived in Indian Territory. The first, Wheelock Mission, was founded by Alfred Wright, a Presbyterian physician, in 1832. During the winter of 1833, the Choctaws began to open their own schools, funded by their annuities. By 1836, they had established eight schools in addition to the eleven mission schools then operating in the Choctaw Nation. In 1843, the Choctaw council also began to provide financial support for boarding schools and Sunday schools. In the latter, adult members of the tribe were instructed in elementary arithmetic and in reading and writing the Choctaw language.

In the early 1840s, Chief Nitakechi returned to Mississippi to encourage his kin to give up their meager existence there and emigrate to Indian Territory. After suffering from poverty, neglect, and continuous pressure to remove for more than a decade, most of the Mississippi Choctaws were eager to join the thriving Choctaw Nation. Between 1845 and 1854, 5,720 Mississippi Choctaws migrated west, 4,523 during the first three years alone. A census taken by BIA agent Douglas H. Cooper in 1853 listed only 2,069 Choctaws in Mississippi and 193 more in Louisiana.

The population of the Choctaw Nation also increased during the 1840s and 1850s because many Chickasaws settled there. The Chickasaws had agreed in 1830 to cede their homeland in northern Mississippi and Alabama to the United States in exchange for land in Indian Territory, shrewdly negotiating for the right to choose this tract themselves. The Chickasaws sent several exploring parties to search for their new western home, but, to the exasperation of the U.S. government, they stalled their removal by continually claiming they could not find any suitable land. In 1833, the Choctaws invited the Chickasaws to settle in their nation in an uninhabited area to the west of the Choctaws' own settlements, but the Chickasaws declined because they did not want to live on lands they did not own. Increasing pressure to remove, however, finally forced them to reconsider. In 1837, they signed the Treaty of Doaksville with the Choctaws, by which the Chickasaws agreed to pay $530,000 for the right to settle in the Choctaw Nation. The next year, the Choctaw council adopted a new constitution that created a fourth governmental district for the Chickasaw immigrants. It also provided for the Chickasaws to elect one chief and nine councilmen to represent them.

Neither the Chickasaws nor the Choctaws were ever comfortable with this arrangement, however. The Chickasaws had little influence in the Choctaw government, because the Choctaws outnumbered them three to one in council. The Choctaws never adjusted to sharing their nation and continued to regard the Chickasaws as intruders in their tribal affairs. Finally, both tribes agreed that the Chickasaws should have their own government. In the Treaty of 1855, which the United States also signed, the Chickasaws were given the right to establish their own council to govern the fourth district, which then became the Chickasaw Nation. The Chickasaws' finances would be kept separate from the Choctaws', but the tribes would hold the title to their lands in common. Citizens of each nation would also have citizenship in the other. In the treaty, the Choctaws also agreed to lease all their land west of the new Chickasaw Nation to the United States for $800,000, half of which would be paid to the Chickasaws. The United States, according to this agreement, was to make this area the permanent home of the Wichita and several other tribes.

The Treaty of 1855 also settled an outstanding dispute between the U.S. government and the Choctaws. The 1830 Treaty of Dancing Rabbit Creek had stated that the Choctaws were entitled to all money received from the sale of their lands in Mississippi, minus the cost of their removal. Although removal expenses totaled approximately $5 million and their Mississippi lands were sold for about $8 million, the United States had not given the profit to the tribe. The Choctaws sent a delegation to Washington, D.C., in 1853 to claim the money, but when they still did not receive a response from the government, the tribe agreed in the 1855 treaty to allow the U.S. Senate to decide its case. In 1859, the Senate awarded the tribe $2,981,247.30, which represented a substantial victory, even though most of the money eventually went toward paying the Choctaws' legal fees.

In the winter of that year, a delegation of Choctaws traveled to North Fork Village in the Creek Nation to meet in council with representatives of the Creek, Cherokee, Seminole, and Chickasaw tribes. At this conference, these Indian tribes adopted a code of laws that would apply to all their people. They also agreed that a citizen of one of their nations could transfer his or her citizenship to another with the approval of the tribal governments involved. The Indian groups that joined this confederation later became known as the *Five Civilized Tribes* because they all had adopted many of the values of white culture.

Although the Choctaws had little contact with eastern settlers during their first three decades in Indian Territory, the tribe's political and social structure came more and more to resemble that of Americans of the period. By 1860, the Choctaws had created the office of principal chief and a supreme court, and had divided their general council into a senate and a house of representatives in deliberate imitation of the U.S. government's executive, judicial, and legislative branches. The tribe's schools at the time enrolled approximately nine hundred students, who were taught in English using a curriculum similar to that of American schools of the day. Many Choctaws also had become Christians. Nearly one-fourth of the Choctaws belonged to the Presbyterian, Methodist, or Baptist Churches by the beginning of the 1860s. Despite these changes from their traditional way of life, however, the Choctaws retained their independence. Left to their own devices, they had tamed a wild and remote frontier in an amazingly short amount of time. But this period of peace and prosperity for the Choctaws would soon end, however, as the United States once again pulled the tribe into its own conflicts at the onset of the American Civil War.

5

The End of a Nation

When the American Civil War broke out in April 1861, tribal leaders hoped they would be able to keep the Choctaw Nation out of the conflict. The Choctaw chiefs immediately declared their neutrality to the commissioner of Indian affairs, but, by June, the tribe had already begun to reconsider its position. Douglas H. Cooper, who had been the Choctaws' agent for eight years and was well regarded by them, was an ardent advocate for the South. His influence helped increase the Choctaws' support for the Confederacy. As slave owners, the Choctaws tended to sympathize with the South, and these leanings were intensified by their disappointment with the U.S. government.

At the beginning of the war, the United States had removed all of its armies from Indian Territory because this large area would require too many soldiers to defend against enemy attack. Without the military protection the United States had guaranteed them in treaty after treaty, the Choctaws were not only vulnerable to Southern troops, but also to hostile white settlers in Arkansas and Texas. The departure of Union forces left the tribe little choice but to ally itself with the Confederacy. On July 12, the Choctaws sent some members of their council to North Fork Village in the Creek Nation to meet with representatives of the Confederate government. There, the Choctaws signed a treaty of allegiance in which the Confederacy promised to protect the Choctaw Nation and respect its independence.

Despite this alliance, few Choctaws actually fought in the Confederate Army. Union forces destroyed the Confederate stores in Perryville and captured the outpost at Skullyville in 1863, but, otherwise, Choctaw lands were not invaded. The Creek and the Cherokee Nations, on the other hand, were occupied by Union troops for the last two years of the war. Confederate troops and refugees from these tribes escaped to Choctaw country, where the needs of the extra population caused a food shortage for the duration of the war. The Choctaws were further impoverished by the loss of their annuity income—the United States had stopped paying annuities to the Choctaws when the tribe allied itself with the Confederacy, and the Confederate government had not provided for the Choctaws' payment as it had promised.

Following the military defeat of the South in April 1865, Chief Peter Pitchlynn surrendered the Choctaws' military forces to the U.S. government on June 19. In September, he led a Choctaw delegation to Fort Smith, Arkansas, where the commissioner of Indian affairs had called a council of all formerly Confederate-allied Indian tribes. Although the delegation was anxious for the Choctaw Nation to resume relations with the United States, it resisted the terms of the peace treaty drafted by the government. In exchange for the protection of the U.S. Army and restoration of the tribal annuities, the Choctaws were expected to abolish slavery, to allow their freed black slaves to remain in their lands, and to surrender one-third

Though only a quarter Choctaw, Peter Pitchlynn was an important liaison between the tribe and the U.S. government. A skillful claims representative, Pitchlynn was able to get the U.S. government to agree to pay the $3 million it owed the Choctaws for the sale of their land in Mississippi and as a result, the Choctaws elected Pitchlynn chief in 1864. Despite the Choctaws siding with the Confederacy during the Civil War, Pitchlynn was able to negotiate a peace settlement with the United States in 1866 that demanded surprisingly few concessions from the tribe.

of their territory, which the government planned to give to Kansas Indians who had supported the Union during the war.

Although the Choctaws accepted a preliminary treaty that included these provisions, the tribe's council instructed the delegation it sent to Washington not to cede any territory occupied by Choctaws in the final treaty. Owing largely to the diplomatic skills of Peter Pitchlynn, the delegation succeeded in not surrendering any tribal territory. It did agree, however, to give up control of the Choctaw lands west of the Chickasaw Nation, which the U.S. government had been leasing since 1855. The United States planned to remove the Choctaws' black population to this area because they objected to their slaves becoming citizens of the Choctaw Nation and thus becoming eligible for a share of their tribal annuities. The U.S. government tried to induce the Choctaws to incorporate the former slaves into their nation by offering the tribe $150,000 for the leased district on the condition that they allow the

(continued on page 54)

Peter Pitchlynn (1806–1881)

Peter Perkins Pitchlynn was born in 1806 to a part-Choctaw mother and an English father. Peter's grandfather, Isaac Pitchlynn, had traveled to Choctaw country in 1774, accompanied by his son John, to trade with the Indians. When Isaac died, John Pitchlynn decided to stay among the Choctaws and married Sophia Folsom. She was the daughter of a Choctaw woman and Nathaniel Folsom, one of three English brothers who had also settled in a Choctaw village in the 1770s.

Although Peter was only one-quarter Indian, his early life in some ways was similar to that of any Choctaw boy. Named *Ha-tchoc-tuck-nee* (Snapping Turtle) by his full-blooded friends, he spent much of his youth hunting and playing Choctaw games. But as John Pitchlynn's son, Peter had much more exposure to the culture of white Americans than did his Choctaw contemporaries. The Pitchlynn trading post was visited by many eastern travelers who came through Choctaw country, and the family often entertained the white traders and missionaries who lived in the area. John Pitchlynn's position as an English interpreter for the Choctaws also brought young Peter into contact with U.S. government officials.

This upbringing proved to be an ideal preparation for Peter Pitchlynn's future career in politics and public service. During the 1820s, the Choctaws began to rely on young men, like Pitchlynn, of mixed white and Indian

Peter Pitchlynn (1806-1881) *(continued from page 51)*

parentage to negotiate treaties for the tribe with the United States. More than most other tribespeople, these men possessed knowledge of both English and the customs of white American society that were necessary to deal effectively with federal officials. Elected to the tribal council in 1826 when he was only twenty years old, Pitchlynn played an important role in drafting the first written Choctaw constitution. He made an even greater contribution in helping to negotiate the 1830 Treaty of Dancing Rabbit Creek in which the tribe ceded its homeland in exchange for land to the west in Indian Territory. Although he vigorously opposed removal, once it appeared inevitable, Pitchlynn shrewdly persuaded Secretary of War John Eaton to make several concessions in the treaty that would benefit the Choctaws.

After the treaty was signed, Pitchlynn's popularity faded. The full-blooded members of the tribe, most of whom did not want to remove to Indian Territory, felt betrayed by their mixed-blooded leaders and accused the treaty negotiators of taking bribes from the federal government. To regain some of his lost favor, Pitchlynn accepted a post as superintendent of the Choctaw Academy in Kentucky in 1841. For several years, the Choctaws, especially the full-bloods, had hoped the federal government would close this eastern boarding school because they believed their children were learning little there other than the vices of white society, particularly drinking and gambling. Using the influence of his position, Pitchlynn convinced officials in Washington, D.C., that the institution he headed was of no value to the tribe. The federal government finally agreed to shut down the school and use the annuity funds that had supported the academy for schools located within the Choctaw Nation. The Choctaws rewarded Pitchlynn by electing him to the tribal council in 1842. Pitchlynn's success in dealing with U.S. officials inspired him to spend more time in Washington. Throughout the late 1840s and the 1850s, he traveled to the capital to make claims on behalf of the Choctaws in Mississippi who had not received the tracts of land that were promised to them in the Treaty of Dancing Rabbit Creek. In many cases, Pitchlynn won cash settlements for the claimants he represented, although he always deducted a substantial fee from the money collected.

Impressed by his skills as a claims representative, the tribe in 1853 selected Pitchlynn to be part of a delegation to present its own claim that the U.S. government owed the Choctaws the $3 million profit from the sale of the tribe's Mississippi lands. After pleading its case in Washington for six years, the delegation triumphed when the Senate agreed in 1859 that the money belonged to the tribe. It was also a personal victory for Pitchlynn, for he had been guaranteed ten percent of any award as his commission.

In 1861, when the outbreak of the Civil War seemed imminent, Pitchlynn returned to Indian Territory. He urged the Choctaws to remain loyal to the Union, possibly because it had not yet paid in full either the 1859 award to the tribe or his commission. Pitchlynn failed to convince the Choctaws, however, and the tribe instead supported the Confederate States, a position Pitchlynn also came to adopt before the war had ended. The Choctaws, however, continued to perceive him as a Yankee (Northern) sympathizer, which, ironically, worked to his political advantage. Anticipating the fall of the Confederacy and seeking a spokesperson who would have influence with the federal government, the Choctaws elected Pitchlynn as their chief in 1864. Their confidence in Pitchlynn was well placed. The Treaty of 1866 established peace between the Choctaws and the United States and demanded surprisingly few concessions from the tribe.

Pitchlynn's tenure as chief was brief. After he lost the election in 1866, he returned to Washington and devoted the rest of his life to securing the funds the U.S. government owed to the tribe according to the 1859 Senate ruling and the 1866 treaty. Pitchlynn did not live to see the outcome of his efforts, however, because the federal government did not pay the money it owed the Choctaws until after his death in 1881. Pitchlynn was buried in Congressional Cemetery in Washington, a non-Indian burial ground. This seemed appropriate, for he had lived most of his adult life in white American society. But it is equally appropriate that Pitchlynn's grave is close to that of the great Choctaw Chief Pushmataha, who had died in Washington while negotiating the Treaty of 1825. Like Pushmataha, Pitchlynn spent his last days far from his homeland in the service of his people.

(continued from page 51)

blacks to settle among them. Although the tribal government was deeply in debt, the council declined the money and asked the commissioner of Indian affairs to proceed with the removal of the freed slaves. When the U.S. government was not able to have its way through negotiation, it tried another tack: The United States simply ignored the request and paid the Choctaws the $150,000 anyway.

The Choctaws themselves wanted to disregard several other provisions in the treaty. One stipulated that the Choctaws were to attend an annual council of all the tribes living in Indian Territory. The U.S. government hoped that it could eventually abolish individual tribal governments and establish this council as the central government over the entire territory, a plan the Choctaws feared and resented because it threatened their nation's independence. The Choctaws also resisted the treaty's specifications for a survey of their lands, which would be used to divide their territory if, in the future, they elected to give up common ownership of their tribal lands. The United States wanted to encourage the Choctaws to section off their territory into individually owned tracts, or *allotments*, but the Choctaws distrusted the program; they remembered how few of their Mississippi kin had received the land promised them by the U.S. government back in 1830.

The provision of the Treaty of 1866 that had the greatest immediate effect on the tribe was the one granting permission for the construction of a railroad across the Choctaw Nation. Even before the treaty was ratified, employees of Kansas railroad companies were racing to the border of Indian Territory. The first to get there was the Missouri-Kansas-Texas Railroad, which was nicknamed "the Katy." Between the summer of 1870 and the spring of 1872, the railroad company built a line running north to south through the Cherokee, Creek, and Choctaw Nations. The Choctaw council became angry because the Katy had paid them nothing for the use of their land. The Choctaws' complaints received little attention, however, especially after 1871, when Congress passed a law stating that railroad companies needed only congressional approval to construct lines through Indian Territory. Many more railroad lines were quickly built, including three additional ones through the Choctaw Nation over the next twenty years.

The coming of the railroads produced some dramatic changes in the Choctaws' way of life. Settlement patterns, for instance, were altered as many new towns sprang up along the new railway routes. Older Choctaw towns and villages that were not near the railroads were virtually abandoned.

The railroads also transformed the economy of the Choctaw Nation. Before the Civil War, some coal had been mined in the area, but only for use by local blacksmiths. The railroads, however, made it easy to transport coal to the East, where there was a strong demand for the mineral to fuel the growing steel industry.

Mine operators soon flocked to the mineral-rich lands of the Choctaws. One of the first of these was J.J. McAlester, a white store owner from Fort Smith, Arkansas. The Choctaw Constitution granted that any citizen who discovered minerals in the Choctaw Nation was entitled to own and operate a mine there. McAlester, who had married a Chickasaw woman and therefore had Choctaw citizenship, formed a company to develop mines in the tribal territory, which he then leased to mine operators for a royalty, or percentage of their profits. When McAlester refused to hand over his royalties to the Choctaw Nation and cited the provision in the constitution, Chief Coleman Cole was outraged and, contrary to the laws of the Choctaw Nation, ordered McAlester's execution. McAlester escaped, and, thereafter, half of the income of all mine owners in Choctaw country was paid to the tribal government.

With the rapid growth of the mining industry, the composition of the population of the Choctaw Nation changed radically. Mines were operated primarily by white men who recently arrived from Europe, including Czechs, Slovaks,

Hungarians, Belgians, Germans, French, English, Swedes, and Italians. As mining increased, American miners from eastern coalfields and African Americans from Texas also immigrated to Indian Territory. The developing lumber industry, made possible by the railroads, attracted additional white workers to Choctaw lands. In 1885, a census of the Choctaw Nation counted 12,816 Indians, 427 whites, and 38 blacks. In 1890, a survey listed 10,017 Indians, 28,345 whites, and 4,406 blacks. Although the tribal income increased greatly because of the new industries, the Choctaw had quickly become outnumbered in their own country.

Despite the overwhelming numbers of newcomers, the Choctaws resisted social contact with both whites and blacks. They preferred to practice many of their traditional customs, and most continued to farm, hunt, and fish for their livelihood. The American customs that most influenced the western Choctaws in the last decades of the nineteenth century were those that had been introduced to them by missionaries before their removal—namely, Christianity and education. Although missionaries had fallen out of favor somewhat with the tribe, their religion had not. The Baptist faith in particular was practiced by a large number of the Choctaws in Indian Territory.

One of the converted, Peter Folsom, traveled to Mississippi to establish a Baptist church there for his fellow Choctaws in 1879. Many other missionaries came to work among the Mississippi Choctaws during this period. After the Civil War, the lives of these Indians had improved as more became *tenant farmers* who rented the fields they worked from landowners, instead of squatters. Yet the Choctaws in Mississippi were still a poor people, and therefore they welcomed the religion and services the missionaries offered them. In Mississippi, there were eight Baptist ministers and nine Baptist churches, which by 1891, served approximately three hundred Choctaws. Methodist and Catholic churches as well as several mission schools were established for these Indians in the late 1890s.

During the Civil War, the Choctaws in Indian Territory had been forced to close their schools because of the lack of tribal funds, but as soon as the annuities were restored, the tribal government began to revive its educational system. It first reopened two of the nation's finest boarding schools—Spencer Academy for boys and New Hope Seminary for girls. As national revenues grew, other boarding schools and neighborhood schools resumed operation, and the council began to send the Choctaws' most promising students to the best American universities. At the end of the nineteenth century, the Choctaw Nation had a much better educated population than any of the states that bordered it. There were also many more literate Indians than whites within the nation, for, as noncitizens, whites were not permitted to attend the tribe's public schools.

Without citizenship, the white inhabitants of the Choctaw Nation were denied other important privileges. Although whites paid taxes to the Choctaw council, they had no representation in it; nor could they own the land on which they built their homes and businesses, because the territory of the nation was still tribally owned. Once they outnumbered the Choctaws, white settlers began to resent that they did not have the right to own land and were not represented in the Choctaw council, and they repeatedly appealed to the U.S. government to dissolve the Choctaw government and the tribal ownership of its land. This pressure increased after 1889, when the United States organized Oklahoma Territory from the western portion of Indian Territory and opened this area to white settlement. Indian Territory was then reduced to only the lands of the Five Civilized Tribes and of the Indian groups who lived in the northeastern corner of the territory under the jurisdiction of the Quapaw Agency.

On March 3, 1893, Congress passed a bill that gave President Grover Cleveland the right to form a committee of commissioners to negotiate the *termination* of the Five Civilized Tribes' land titles, either by persuading the Indians to allot their territory to individuals or to cede it to the United States. The resulting committee, known as the Dawes Commission after committee chairman Henry L. Dawes, first approached the Choctaws in February 1894 with a proposal for the allotment of land in the Choctaw Nation. The tribe rejected the plan, but when the commission persisted, the Choctaws organized a committee of three who spoke both English and Choctaw to escort the U.S. commissioners on a tour of the nation. The tribe hoped that once the Dawes Commission witnessed the Choctaws' progress and heard firsthand the people's resistance to allotment, it would leave the tribe alone. The commissioners, however, did not appear to appreciate the tribe's attachment to its institutions and merely pressed the Choctaw leaders even harder to negotiate.

As it became obvious that the Dawes Commission would not give up, some Choctaws began to favor allotment. They feared the U.S. government might take their land by force if the tribe did not cooperate. The leader of this faction was Green McCurtain, who was elected principal chief of the tribe in the fall of 1895. Although most Choctaws still opposed allotment, this majority split its votes among three other candidates who all supported preserving tribal ownership of their lands.

Against the wishes of the majority of the Choctaws, McCurtain formed a committee of nine council members, including himself, to negotiate with the Dawes Commission soon after the election. The committee met with the commissioners in December at the town of Muskogee in the Cherokee Nation and there agreed to give the United States title to the Choctaws' and Chickasaws' territory. The United States was to divide this land equally among all the citizens of these Indian nations, except for the former black slaves who would receive only forty acres. The land occupied by towns and public buildings would be sold, and all citizens, excluding blacks, would be given a share of the proceeds. Mines within the nations' territory would also be sold, but the U.S. government was to use the money to support schools in the area. The tribal government would stay in place until March 1905 to oversee the allotment process.

The Choctaw committee signed an agreement at Muskogee on December 18, but the Chickasaw council rejected the plan, and Congress refused to ratify the agreement without the Chickasaws' approval. In April, McCurtain and his committee met with Chickasaw representatives in Atoka in the Pushmataha District to try to convince the two tribes of the wisdom of allotment. McCurtain succeeded and the two tribes drafted the Atoka Agreement with the United States. Aside from a few administrative details, it called for the same allotment program as described in the Muskogee document.

As soon as the Atoka Agreement was signed, the Dawes Commission set about compiling a roll that would list everyone entitled to an allotment. This process was complicated when many people who claimed to be Choctaw—but who had never lived in and were not citizens of the Choctaw Nation—applied for an allotment. In 1900, Congress passed legislation declaring that these applications were not valid, although it did make an exception for Choctaws in Mississippi. The law stated that Mississippi Choctaws were entitled to an allotment if they agreed to live on the land granted them and if they could prove they were descendants of the Choctaws who had requested tracts in their homeland according to the terms of the 1830 Treaty of Dancing Rabbit Creek. Colonel William Ward, the agent who had the responsibility of registering these requests, had left very poor records, however. Unable to verify the claimants' descent, the U.S. government was flooded with more than six thousand applications for allotment, most of which were fraudulent. Many of the actual descendants refused to come forward because they were afraid that the promise of tracts of land in Indian Territory was just another scheme by the U.S. government to steal their Mississippi homes. At least

Green McCurtain (left) with fellow members of the Choctaw Council: Victor M. Locke, Peter J. Hudson, and Dr. E.N. Wright. McCurtain served as principal chief of the Choctaws from 1896 to 1900 and again from 1902 until his death in 1910. A proponent of allotment, McCurtain signed the Atoka Agreement in 1898, which called for both Choctaw and Chickasaw land in Oklahoma to be divided into individual parcels among members of the tribes.

three hundred did travel west by train to claim their allotments in 1903, and others were later brought to Indian Territory by land speculators who were eager to cheat the Indians out of the land they would receive.

The African Americans in the Choctaw Nation further complicated the work of the Dawes Commission by objecting to the forty-acre limit placed on their allotments by the Atoka Agreement. Many claimed they had one Choctaw parent or grandparent and therefore were eligible for as large a tract of land as other mixed-blooded Choctaw citizens. Although the

Senate sent a committee to investigate these claims in 1906, the U.S. government closed the tribal rolls on March 4, 1907, with many disputes still outstanding. The final roll listed 18,981 Indian citizens of the Choctaw Nation, 1,639 Mississippi Choctaws, and 5,994 former black slaves.

Throughout the long allotment process, the white settlers in the Choctaw Nation had been eager for the creation of a local government in which they would be represented. The Atoka Agreement had provided that the Choctaw government would stay in place until March 1905, but, because the roll had taken much longer to compile than expected, this date was extended to April 1906. After all tribal governments were dissolved, the United States planned to merge Indian Territory and the newly formed Oklahoma Territory into one state. The Choctaws made one last attempt to maintain some control over their lands by sending delegates to a conference of representatives of the Five Civilized Tribes in Muskogee in July 1905. There, the Indians drew up a constitution for a separate state that would be formed from the lands of Indian Territory only. The tribes decided to name their state Sequoyah in honor of the Cherokee leader who had invented his tribe's written language. (For additional information on these five Indian tribes that were forcibly removed from their homelands to Oklahoma, enter "Five Civilized Tribes" into any search engine and browse the many sites listed.)

Congress refused to acknowledge the document, however, and, on November 16, 1907, eight months after the tribal roll was compiled, the Choctaws became citizens of the state of Oklahoma. Despite decades of the tribe's constant efforts to preserve its independence, the Choctaw Nation had come to an end.

6

A
Divided
People
Continues

In the 1830s, the U.S. government had removed Indians to territory in the West to accommodate white settlers on the homelands of eastern tribes. In the 1880s, when settlers hungered for the Indians' new territory, the government proposed dividing Indian land into individually owned allotments as its new solution. The United States hoped that allotment would free this territory for white settlement as well as encourage Indians to become farmers and assimilate into the non-Indian mainstream society. This would at last relieve the federal government of having to deal with a large population within its borders who did not share the culture of the majority of Americans.

After the Choctaws received their allotments, many quickly sold their land, often for less than its actual value, to white land speculators. The government attempted to discourage such sales but was largely unsuccessful, and most Choctaws lost their original allotments of land. The Choctaws soon scattered across Oklahoma, and, as the

Cane splint "Elbow" basket, c. 1980; made by Elsie Battiest, Oklahoma, Museum of The Red River, Idabel, Oklahoma.

Cane splint bowl basket, c. 1950, Mississippi, Museum of The Red River, Idabel, Oklahoma.

Cane splint "Heart" or friendship basket, c. 1920, Oklahoma, Museum of The Red River, Idabel, Oklahoma.

Corn grater, early twentieth century, Oklahoma, Museum of The Red River, Idabel, Oklahoma. A homemade punched sheet of tin nailed to a plank; used to scrape green corn of the cob for making hominy.

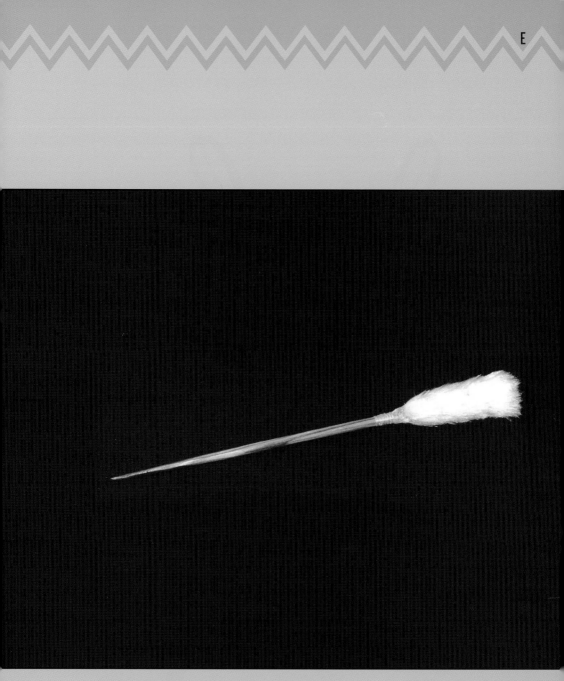

Dart for a blowgun, c. 1980, Museum of The Red River, Idabel, Oklahoma. Arrow shaft is pine splint with thistledown.

Ball sticks, c. 1955; made by Sidney Wright, Eagletown, Oklahoma; Ball, c. 1980, Mississippi; Museum of The Red River, Idabel, Oklahoma.

Choctaw traditional dress for a five-year-old girl, c. 2000, Oklahoma, Museum of The Red River, Idabel, Oklahoma.

Choctaw shirt for a four- or five-year-old boy, c. 2002, Mississippi, Museum of The Red River, Idabel, Oklahoma.

government had hoped, they lost much of their tribal unity as a result.

The Choctaws in Oklahoma adopted many American customs and habits but most continued to farm, largely planting cotton and corn. However, much of the best farmland in the former Choctaw Nation had been sold to non-Indians, making it too difficult for the Choctaws to continue to farm. With their traditional means of earning a living gone, many of the Oklahoma Choctaws began to take jobs in the timber and mining industries and, later, in manufacturing.

Although their tribal government had been dissolved in 1906, the federal government still allowed the Choctaws in Oklahoma to maintain a principal chief to conduct certain ongoing tribal affairs. Instead of being elected, however, the principal chiefs, following allotment, were appointed by the president of the United States and served under the supervision of the Bureau of Indian Affairs (BIA). One of the major tasks that faced the first several appointed principal chiefs was to press the U.S. government to sell the tribe's public land and distribute the income to the Choctaw people as specified by the Atoka Agreement. By 1920, all enrolled Choctaws or their heirs had at last received approximately $1,070 each from land sales. However, the government did not make payments on the sale of their mineral reserves until 1949.

When the Dawes Commission had closed its tribal roll book in 1907, more than a thousand Choctaws remained in Mississippi. Unlike their Oklahoma kin, the Mississippi Choctaws were able to retain their group identity and many of their traditional customs, yet most continued to live in poverty. After nearly eighty years of ignoring the suffering of this branch of the tribe, Congress investigated the living conditions of the Choctaws in Mississippi in 1908 and 1916. The findings convinced Secretary of the Interior Franklin Lane, who was now overseeing the Bureau of Indian Affairs, and President Woodrow Wilson that the Mississippi Choctaws needed help.

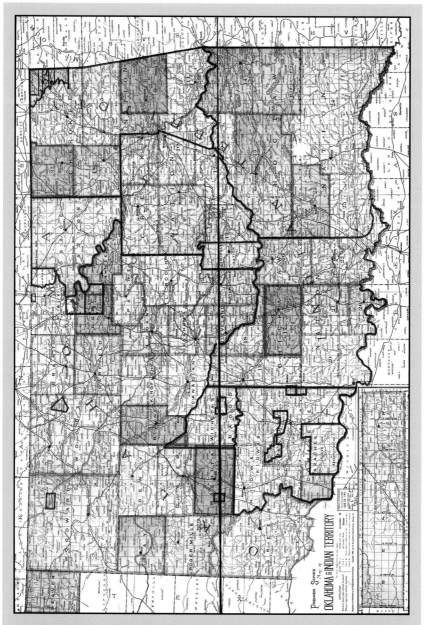

A map of Oklahoma and Indian Territory, c. 1905, two years before Oklahoma entered the Union as the 46th state. The Choctaws held much of the southeastern part of what is now Oklahoma; an area that consisted of approximately thirteen million acres and stretched from the Red River in the south to the Arkansas and Canadian Rivers in the north.

In 1918, the BIA established the Choctaw Indian Agency in Philadelphia, Mississippi, to direct various programs aimed at improving the general welfare of the members of the tribe in the state. Initially, the government authorized a budget of $75,000, which the agency allocated in equal parts for farmland, farm supplies, and education. In 1920, the agency started a program for the establishment of day schools, and within fifteen years, there was an elementary school in each of the Mississippi Choctaws' seven communities: Pearl River, Conehatta, Bogue Chitto, Redwater, Tucker, Standing Pine, and Bogue Homa. The agency also launched a land-purchase program in 1921 through which the federal government, on behalf of the Choctaws, bought land in Neshoba County, where most of the Choctaws lived, and in three neighboring counties settled by the tribe.

The aid provided to the Mississippi Choctaws reflects the changing policy of the U.S. government toward the American Indian in the 1920s. In 1926, the secretary of the interior commissioned a study of the Bureau of Indian Affairs. It concluded that the United States had not acted responsibly when it dissolved tribal governments and allotted Indian land without providing Native people with the education or job training they needed to prosper economically. In 1934, Congress put the proposals made in this report into action by passing the *Indian Reorganization Act* (Wheeler-Howard Act), which prohibited further allotment of land, permitted the organization of new tribal governments, and attempted to reverse the trend of having BIA *reservation* superintendents serve as the center of government on various Indian reservations. The enactment of the reforms advocated in the Indian Reorganization Act helped to usher in an era of growth for the American Indian nationally. The Mississippi and Oklahoma Choctaws benefited from this act, but still the BIA exercised a very powerful influence, and the Choctaws had virtually no control over their programs and services.

This left them ill-equipped to influence community and *economic development.*

As a result, the Oklahoma Choctaws formed a delegation consisting of one representative from each of the ten counties in the area that had at one time made up the Choctaw Nation. This delegation met at the Goodland Indian School near Hugo, Oklahoma, in 1934 and established an Advisory Council—the first since their government was dissolved in 1906.

On August 1, 1953, the U.S. government reversed its policy toward Native Americans when Congress passed the Termination Act (House Concurrent Resolution 108). The intent of this resolution was to terminate the federal government's involvement with Indian tribes on reservations throughout the country. The government hoped to free Native Americans from federal supervision and to abolish the Bureau of Indian Affairs. The policy of termination urged Indian tribes to manage their own affairs and to change their traditional institutions and culture to be more like those of modern American society. Thus, the legislation sought to put an end to schools, health clinics, and hospitals operated for Indians alone, as well as to tribal governments. Although most Indian groups liked the idea of self-rule, they did not interpret termination as ending the identity and existence of their group as a legal entity. Principal Chief Harry "Jimmy" Belvin, who, in 1948, was appointed by President Harry S. Truman as principal chief of the Oklahoma Choctaws, was strongly opposed to any proposals that would have terminated the tribe or dissolved the office of principal chief. Belvin worked very diligently to bring an end to the U.S. government's policy of termination. The following year Belvin was elected principal chief, a position he held until 1975 when C. David Gardner was elected principal chief.

Sadly, David Gardner died in January 1978 after a long battle with cancer. As a result, a special election was conducted in April 1978, and Hollis E. Roberts was elected principal chief. Roberts accomplished many things during his administration; the most important of which was the adoption of a modern constitution in 1983, which was ratified by the people on June 9, 1984. He also enacted legislation to change the title "principal chief" to simply "chief." The updated constitution provided for an executive, legislative, and judicial branch of government. The chief is elected every four years and the legislative authority of the tribe is vested in the tribal council, which consists of twelve members—one each from the twelve districts in the Choctaw Nation that includes a ten and a half county area in Southeast Oklahoma. The chief is not a voting member of the council, but he or she has the authority to appoint an assistant chief with the advice and consent of the tribal council.

The Mississippi Choctaws also went through some major changes during the twentieth century. In 1944, Harold L. Ickes, the U.S. secretary of the interior, announced that the 15,150 acres of land the federal government had purchased for the Mississippi Choctaws would be converted into a reservation. The following year, the secretary sanctioned the adoption of a constitution and bylaws that officially established the Mississippi Band of Choctaw Indians. The Mississippi Choctaws were then formally recognized by the United States and were able to organize their own tribal government. They established the office of tribal chairman, who would be appointed by a sixteen-member council elected from the seven communities of Bogue Chitto, Bogue Homa, Conehatta, Pearl River, Redwater, Standing Pine, and Tucker, with the number of representatives from each community allotted in proportion to the population. Although the seven communities are located in a four-county area in eastern Mississippi, the reservation now contains some thirty-five thousand acres spread over ten different counties. Pearl River is the largest community and is the site of tribal government headquarters.

The Mississippi Choctaws were also affected by termination as the U.S. government put this policy into action in Mississippi by establishing various vocational training programs to prepare the Choctaws to take jobs off the reservation. Some Choctaws received training on the reservation, but others moved to the major cities of Chicago, Cleveland, and Dallas to attend special vocational training centers. Although many Choctaws participated in these programs and some moved to cities to seek employment once they had learned a trade, most preferred to remain on the reservation despite the relative lack of jobs and the government's efforts to remove them.

In the 1960s, the administrations of Presidents John F. Kennedy and Lyndon B. Johnson concluded that Native Americans would be better served by a federal policy that encouraged *self-determination*—one that would allow them to decide whether to remain on their reservations or to move to towns and cities where they would be more likely to adopt the culture of mainstream America. Johnson, in an address to the U.S. Senate on March 6, 1968, proposed "a policy expressed in programs of self-help, self-development, and self-determination." On September 22, 1968, Congress passed Senate Concurrent Resolution 11, which was an effort to replace House Concurrent Resolution 108. In 1968, Congress also passed the Indian Civil Rights Act (Public Law 90-184), which was designed for reservation Indians. New goals were established in this act that included raising the standard of living for Native Americans.

During these presidential administrations, Congress again passed various acts and programs to aid the economic and social development of Native Americans. This policy continued in the years that followed with legislation of the Indian Education and Self-Determination Act (1975), which called for "maximum Indian participation in the government and education of the Indian people; provide for the

full participation of Indian tribes in programs and services conducted by the federal government for Indians and to encourage
the development of human resources of the Indian people;
establish a program of assistance to upgrade Indian education;
support the right of Indians to control their own educational
activities; and for other purposes."

Since the initial introduction of the self-determination
policy, the Choctaws on the Mississippi reservation have
greatly improved their economy. To provide job opportunities for their people, Choctaw leaders established the
Choctaw Development Enterprise in 1969. The company has
built or repaired numerous homes on the reservation and
has constructed several community centers and tribal
offices. In 1973, it completed an industrial park at Pearl
River, which has attracted many corporations that are now
headquartered on the reservation. In 1977, Chief Phillip
Martin was instrumental in persuading the Packard Electric
Division of the General Motors Corporation to establish the
Chata Wire Harness Enterprise in Pearl River. This company
employs many Choctaws who assemble electrical parts for
some of the cars manufactured by General Motors. Several
other plants have also opened in the park since the 1980s,
including the Choctaw Greeting Enterprise of the American
Greeting Corporation, where Choctaw workers assemble
greeting cards; and the Choctaw Electronics Enterprise of
the Oxford Investment Company of Chicago, where Choctaws
manufacture automobile radio speakers. (For additional information on this enterprising Mississippi Choctaw chief, enter
"Choctaw Chief Phillip Martin" into any search engine and
browse the many sites listed.)

The many jobs created for the Choctaws by the firms in
the industrial park have spurred recent efforts by the tribal
leadership to seek additional companies willing to locate plants
in nearby Choctaw communities. In 1986, as a result of these
efforts to encourage investment, new plants were opened in

nearby DeKalb County and in the town of Carthage, near the Choctaw community of Redwater. First American Printing and Direct Mail, located in Ocean Springs on the Mississippi Gulf Coast, was acquired in 1992. This facility provides printing, data management, direct mail, and telemarketing services for a nationally based clientele. In 1994, First American Plastics opened a facility in Ocean Springs that manufactures plastic injection molding used to make cutlery. Today, the Choctaw tribe operates several high-tech businesses and produces many products, including plastic cutlery for fast-food chains like McDonald's and wiring components for Caterpillar, Club Car, Inc., and Ford Power Products.

In addition to establishing manufacturing jobs, the Mississippi Choctaw leaders attempted to diversify their economy by improving the retail, service, and government sectors through the creation of enterprises such as a shopping center and a nursing home on the reservation.

However, efforts to improve the economy changed dramatically after the Indian Gaming Regulatory Act was passed by Congress in 1988. The act allowed the Choctaws to set up casinos on the reservation, and in 1994, they opened Silver Star Resort and Casino, which employs more than two thousand people and generates revenue that helps support an array of tribal programs. Due to Silver Star's success, the Choctaws expanded their tourism industry by opening the Dancing Rabbit Golf Club in 1997, and the Geyser Falls Water Theme Park and the Golden Moon Hotel and Casino in 2002. More hotels, retail shopping, and additional golf courses are currently in various stages of development.

Today, the Mississippi Band of Choctaw Indians operate approximately twenty-two businesses and is the majority owner of three joint ventures that employ more than nine thousand people. Some sixty percent of the tribe's employees are non-Indian and more than fifty percent of those who are employed are engaged in the gaming industry. Many other

Choctaws hold positions with various tribal agencies and all but a few have abandoned farming as a means to earn a living. Many Choctaws also have jobs off the reservation. Although the average income of the Choctaws has risen substantially in recent years, it still remains below regional and national averages. However, the unemployment rate is consistently below the national average and only about three percent of Choctaws rely on welfare. Thus, the quality of life for most Choctaws is much better now than it was forty years ago, when ninety percent of the Choctaw population lived in poverty.

The number of Choctaws living in Mississippi during the past several decades has also steadily increased. Between 1960 and 1980, the state's Choctaw population grew from 3,119 to 6,313. By 2000, it had increased to 11,652. The reservation population in 1982 numbered 4,398, approximately sixty percent of whom were under twenty-five years of age. By 1990, the number of people living on the reservation had increased to 4,449.

As of 2004, more than 9,100 persons are enrolled as members of the Mississippi Band of Choctaw Indians. Registered tribal members must be at least one-half Mississippi Choctaw. About six thousand members of the population live on the reservation. A tribal demographic survey taken of the tribe in 1990 revealed that 83.6 percent were full-blooded and 14.5 percent had at least a 50 percent quantum degree of Choctaw blood. About fifty percent were under the age of twenty-one.

Most of the children on the reservation attend elementary schools in their communities or go to the Choctaw Central High School, which was built in 1963 at Pearl River. The median grade completed in 1968 was sixth, but by 1975, it had increased to eighth grade. By 1990, the educational level achieved by most Choctaw students had reached the eleventh grade. Although the majority of the Choctaw people now speak both Choctaw and English, a study conducted in the 1980s indicated that only about fifty-eight percent of the population could speak English well and only about fifty percent were skilled in writing the language. To combat these problems, the U.S. government established adult literacy programs at Pearl River, which have helped many Choctaws earn eighth-grade education certificates and high school diplomas. In addition, the Choctaws have constructed many new schools and early childhood centers on the reservation to help upgrade educational attainment.

The Mississippi Choctaws are also working to provide better health care for their people. Infectious diseases, particularly pneumonia and tuberculosis, are the leading cause of death among the Choctaws; therefore, their health-service programs aim to educate them about preventive medicine, proper nutrition, and the elimination of environmental health hazards. The Choctaw Health Center, a forty-three-bed hospital opened in 1976, and a nursing home constructed in the 1980s have helped to improve health-care services. Smaller health clinics are also in operation in Choctaw communities such as Bogue Chitto, Conehatta, and Redwater.

The quality of housing for the Choctaws in Mississippi has improved throughout the twentieth century. During the 1930s, about two hundred small wood homes were built through a federal housing construction program. Very few new homes were constructed on the reservation until 1965, when the Choctaw Housing Authority (CHA) was established. This organization was initially responsible for the building of about two hundred houses. By 1995, CHA had built almost a thousand houses and many more are currently under construction or are being planned for the future. These brick homes have many of the same modern conveniences found in most homes throughout the rest of the country today.

The Choctaws presently living on the reservation still have their own tribal government, although its structure is different from the system organized in 1945. In 1975, the Choctaws

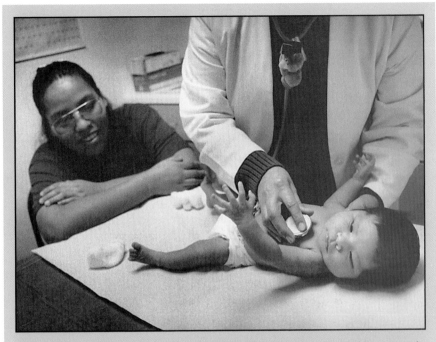

The Choctaw Health Center, located in Philadelphia, Mississippi, opened in 1976 and is a fully accredited medical facility that includes a twenty-four-hour emergency medical services department, outpatient and dental clinics, a mental health center, a diabetes clinic, a disability clinic, a women's wellness center, and a variety of preventative programs. Here, a nurse practitioner examines a newborn.

adopted a revised constitution which changed the title of the executive leader from chairman to chief and called for this official to be elected by the members of the entire tribe to a four-year term rather than being appointed by the council for two years. The Choctaw government has the right to establish its own laws and judicial system; therefore, the state of Mississippi has no political power over the reservation. The tribal council now meets on the second Tuesday of January, April, July, and October of each year to discuss tribal matters, although additional special meetings may be called by the chief. The federal government, however, is ultimately responsible for the protection of the Choctaws and the tribe's property from encroachment by the state and its citizens.

Although the Choctaw government in Oklahoma owns several tracts of land, these landholdings are not organized as a reservation. The council of the western branch of the Choctaws does have the power to make tribal laws, but the Oklahoma Choctaws also must adhere to the laws of the state. Their tribal government has played a tremendous role in the lives of the Choctaws in recent years. Just as self-determination and the passage of the National Indian Gaming Act have allowed their Mississippi kin to flourish, these policies have helped the Choctaw government in Durant, Oklahoma, to administer many programs and establish institutions to improve the health, education, and income of its people.

In 1987, the Oklahoma Choctaws built the Choctaw Bingo Parlor south of Durant. Revenue generated from this enterprise was then used to start the Choctaw Finishing Company and to open the nearby Choctaw Travel Plaza and Smoke Shop in 1990. The Choctaw Travel Plaza has subsequently been expanded and the Choctaw Nation now operates twelve travel plazas and smoke shops in Atoka, Broken Bow, Durant (East) and (West), Garvin, Hugo, Idabel, McAlester, Pecola, Poteau, Stringtown, and Wilburton. In addition, it runs six gaming casinos located in Durant, Idabel, Pocola, McAlester, Stringtown, and Hugo. The Choctaws also own manufacturing plants in Hugo and McAlester and they are attempting to further diversify their economy so they can be less dependent upon the gaming industry. Revenue generated from the tribe's various economic endeavors is used to help fund various federal- and Choctaw-sponsored programs and to provide numerous services. For example, some of the educational programs include the Higher Education Scholarship program, which gives financial assistance to enrolled members of the Choctaw tribe who are attending colleges or universities, the Adult Education Program, Head Start (there are fourteen Head Start centers within the Choctaw Nation), Upward Bound (a program designed to assist high school students preparing for college), Clothing Allowance (a one-time payment to students who have completed their first semester of college with passing grades), Vocational Development, the Choctaw Nation Language Program, and the operation of Jones Academy (a residential care center for elementary and secondary school-age children).

With regard to health care, the Choctaw Nation operates a hospital and clinic in Talihina and has other outpatient clinics in Broken Bow, Durant, Hugo, McAlester, and Poteau. The Choctaws also have a Behavioral Health Program, a Diabetes Wellness Center, a Recovery Center, and a Mail Order Pharmacy.

The Choctaws operate seven day-care centers, a Children and Family Services program, Boys and Girls Clubs, a nursing home, and numerous housing programs available through the Choctaw Nation Housing Authority to assist Choctaws in obtaining affordable housing.

To be eligible to participate in the various programs and services provided by the Choctaw Nation, a person must have a Certificate of Degree of Indian Blood (CDIB) card. To obtain a card, a person must be able to verify that he or she is a "descendant of a Dawes Commission enrollee." There are no blood quantum requirements necessary for obtaining a card. By the late 1970s, more than twenty-five thousand persons nationwide held CDIB cards, and by 1993, this number had increased to more than seventy-seven thousand.

The Choctaws in both Oklahoma and Mississippi have retained much of their cultural heritage. Many programs exist that are aimed at helping Choctaws learn how to read and write in the native Choctaw language. The people continue to perform many of their ancient tribal songs and dances, and, after centuries of play, stickball and archery competitions remain popular. Some Choctaw women still weave baskets and make traditional clothing. Handmade Choctaw dresses, frequently worn by older women, require up to six yards of fabric for the skirt alone. Men's shirts for special occasions are usually decorated with intricate beadwork and trimmed with ribbon. Men also often wear ribboned belts and black felt hats.

The Choctaws' traditional customs and costumes are displayed every summer at the Mississippi Choctaws' Indian

The Choctaw Language

Linguists, scholars who study the structure and evolution of human speech, have identified 221 different languages spoken by Indians in North America. These languages can be grouped into several linguistic families by similarities in their grammatical structures. Tribes whose languages come from the same linguistic family do not necessarily live in the same region or share other cultural characteristics, but anthropologists believe that similarities between the languages of two different groups indicate that their ancestors may have belonged to a single group that spoke an early form of these languages in prehistoric times.

The Choctaw language belongs to the Muskogean linguistic family, which also includes the languages of several tribes, such as the Creek and Chickasaw, who were the Choctaws' neighbors in both Mississippi and Indian Territory. Because the sounds of Muskogean languages are very similar to those of English, the Choctaw language can be represented with the Roman alphabet. This fact, combined with the Choctaws' thirst for education, made it easy for Choctaw adults and children to learn to read and write in their language. Within a generation after their removal, most Choctaws were literate.

For this reason, the first missionaries to establish schools among the Choctaws in Indian Territory were able to translate their religious and educational materials and print them in Choctaw. The missionary who was perhaps most responsible for the tribe's quick rate of becoming literate was Presbyterian minister Cyrus Byington. Byington translated many hymns, the New Testament, and most of the Old Testament into Choctaw and compiled the first grammar and dictionary in the language. Aided by the staff of the American Board of Commissioners for Foreign Missions, he also published a tremendous number of tracts in Choctaw, including lectures on morality,

Fair, which has been held annually since 1949 to promote tourism. Each year, more than twenty thousand people come to the campus of the Choctaw High School in Pearl River to attend the event. Many leading national entertainers perform at the fair, helping to make it one of the most popular tourist

biographies of Christian Indians, and Bible stories for children. In 1837 alone, his output totaled more than 576,000 pages of text.

Although classes in the Choctaws' schools were conducted in English, the Choctaw language, both written and spoken, remained an important means of communication, especially among adults, throughout the history of the Choctaw Nation. The many newspapers published in the Choctaw Nation in the late nineteenth century all contained columns and news written in Choctaw, even though the papers were operated by and for the increasing population of non-Indians. To combat the bias of these publications, *Indian Citizen* was established in 1889. Owned and operated by Choctaw tribal members, it was exclusively devoted to the concerns of the tribe. Each issue included local news, editorials, and reports from Washington, D.C., as well as some lively gossip. For less-educated Choctaws who could not read English, *Indian Citizen* was also translated into Choctaw and it published all the treaties the Choctaws had made with the United States and all federal laws pertaining to the tribe.

Today, many Choctaws speak both English and Choctaw. Their native language is preserved in the names of cities, towns, counties, and rivers throughout Mississippi and Oklahoma. The word *Oklahoma* itself is derived from the Choctaw words *okla*, "people," and *homma*, "red." The area was first called Oklahoma by Choctaw Chief Allen Wright in 1866, when he was asked what he would name Indian Territory if the United States succeeded in organizing it under one Indian government.

On the following page, there is a list of additional place names that were adapted from Choctaw words, along with a key to their pronunciation and their original meaning.

The Choctaw Language *(continued from page 77)*

PLACE NAME	PRONUNCIATION	MEANING
Bogue Chitto	bow guh chit tuh	big creek
Bogue Homa	bow guh hoe muh	red creek
Coahoma	kuh hoe muh red	wildcat
Conehatta	ko nuh hat uh	gray skunk
Escatawpa	es kuh taw puh	beaver dam
Homochitto	hoe muh chih tuh	big red
Itta Bena	it uh bee nuh	wood camp
Neshoba	nuh show buh	wolf
Noxubee	knock shuh bee	fishy smell
Ofahoma	oh fuh hoe muh	red dog
Okalona	oak uh loan uh	people got there
Okatibbee	oak uh tih bee	water fight
Panola	puh no luh	cotton
Shubuta	shoe boo tuh	snake
Shuqualak	shug uh lock	crawfish hole
Tchula	chew luh	fox
Yalabusha	yal luh buh shuh	tadpole

attractions in Mississippi. The Choctaws also convene in Tuskahoma, Oklahoma, every Labor Day for an annual festival. At both yearly events, many Choctaws, who today reside in Mississippi, Oklahoma, Louisiana, Alabama, Tennessee, Texas, California, Washington, and other states, gather to celebrate their common heritage. Together again, the Choctaws join in their traditional games and dances and share with the youngest members of the tribe their stories of the long-divided Choctaw people.

7

Into the Twenty-First Century

Today, there are 557 Indian tribes that are located in 33 states across the United States. Alaska, one of the most diverse states, has 226 tribes. According to the 2000 U.S. census, the Native American population is approximately 2.48 million, with 1.3 million living on reservations. Also in 2000, the state of Oklahoma had a total population of 3,450,654, of which 273,230 persons identified themselves as American Indian. However, when persons who claimed to be American Indian alone or in combination with one or more other races were added, then the total increased to 391,949 for 11.4 percent of the total population. Mississippi's Choctaw population in 2000 was 11,652, which amounted to 0.4 percent of the state's population of 2,844,658.

In 2000, the Choctaw Nation in Oklahoma (i.e., Choctaw Tribal Statistical Area, as the U.S. Census Bureau describes it) had a population of 224,472. Of that total, approximately eighteen percent of the people identified themselves as American Indian alone or in combination with one or more other races. Most of the American Indian population of the Choctaw Nation is Choctaw. Thus, it is estimated that approximately 40,404 persons within the Choctaw Nation have identified themselves as having Choctaw heritage. In the 2000 U.S. census, persons identifying themselves as Choctaw alone (not in combination with one or more races) totaled 87,349. Of that number, 11,690 identified themselves as Oklahoma Choctaw, with the remainder living in other states in the United States. Aside from the census, officials of the Choctaw Nation of Oklahoma estimate that the Choctaw Nation has an enrolled membership of more than 130,000.

Native Americans are one of the fastest growing and youngest minorities in the United States. Forty percent of the national Indian population is under twenty years of age. But the American Indian is also one of the poorest, least healthy, and worst educated ethnic minorities in the country. Socioeconomic indicators that measure quality of life and economic development show that the American Indian frequently falls below the national norm in most evaluative categories. Unemployment on many reservations is around fifty percent. Median household income is well below the national average and more than twenty-five percent of American Indians live below the poverty line. Life expectancy is also much lower for Native Americans than the national average.

The various American Indian tribes are diligently working to improve the quality of life of their people. Many tribes see economic development as a key to improving the lifestyle and socioeconomic well-being of its tribal members. The development of high-tech industries and expansion in retail, tourism, and other industries are seen as vital factors that can contribute to overall growth and progress. Generating economic wealth has enabled various tribes to divert revenue into much-needed education, health, and social programs.

Certainly the Mississippi and Oklahoma Choctaws recognize that economic development is vital to their prosperity and have made great progress in this area beginning in the latter quarter of the twentieth century.

One shining example of this dedication is reflected by Chief Phillip Martin, who has helped lift the Mississippi Choctaws out of poverty. Less than a generation ago, the Choctaws had an unemployment rate of nearly eighty percent; now that number stands at less than four percent. The Choctaws' influence on Mississippi's economy has been ever greater—the tribe is currently among the state's five largest employers; its overall contribution to the state economy exceeds $1.2 billion; and more than 8,000 jobs have been created, sixty percent of which are held by non-Choctaws. Martin is proud of the success his people have enjoyed in recent years, saying: "We should be considered the ultimate locally owned business. We live in Mississippi, earn our living in Mississippi, and invest our money in Mississippi. We are not going to move to greener pastures like some companies do. I look forward to continuing our progress, and I like the fact that Mississippi benefits as well. I see nothing but tremendous opportunities for us both."

Gains made in the last quarter of the twentieth century have most certainly given the Choctaws the impetus needed to thrive in the twenty-first century. Growth and change can be measured statistically in many ways. Not only do the Mississippi Choctaws operate more than twenty-two businesses that include printing, plastic molding, greeting cards, and wiring component plants, but they are also moving into more high-tech (e.g., Choctaw Geo Imaging Enterprises) and resort industries. Their business relationships include partnerships with such major U.S. corporations as Ford Motor Company, General Motors, Daimler-Chrysler, Caterpillar, Club Car, American Greetings, Delphi Packard, Matrix Systems, Valeo Sylvania, Federal Mogal, Bergstrom, Navistar International, PepsiCo, Blue Dot, Harman International, and McDonald's restaurants.

Chief Phillip Martin of the Mississippi Band of Choctaw Indians has done a remarkable job of helping to lift his people out of poverty. Since becoming chief in 1979, he has created thousands of jobs for the Choctaws and has reduced their unemployment rate to less than four percent.

One of the most successful business ventures for the Mississippi Choctaws has been the Choctaw Resort Development ment Enterprise (CRDE). Established in 1999, the CRDE is charged with making the Choctaw Reservation a word-class gaming and entertainment destination. The CRDE oversees the Pearl River Resort in Choctaw, Mississippi, which includes Silver Star Resort & Casino, Dancing Rabbit Golf Club, and the Golden Moon Hotel & Casino. The Pearl River Resort, which also includes one of the South's largest water parks, brings in approximately six million visitors a year and generated revenue of $151.6 million over the last quarter of 2003 and the first quarter of 2004.

The success of the resort was reflected in a statement made by Jay Dorris, president of the CRDE, in February 2004: "After a full year of operations at Golden Moon [Casino], we are pleased to see continued increases in net revenues, along with reductions in our costs and expenses resulting from increased efficiencies and cost control measures we implemented. . . . It has been another strong quarter with increasing stability in our revenue and predictability in our expenses as Pearl River Resort continues to gain market share as a must-see resort destination."

With the revenue generated from its numerous economic ventures, the Choctaws are able to invest additional monies into education, health care, housing, job training, and numerous other community services. Though economic success has brought prosperity to the Choctaws, preserving and promoting the tribe's language and culture—through various programs— remains a top priority for both groups. Having a reservation helps foster cohesion within the Choctaw community and to promote its language and culture via its schools, communities, and the Internet. Most older adults speak the Choctaw tongue; however, younger Choctaws are less fluent in the native language. Promoting and preserving its language, the tribe's traditional music and dances, and other features of the Choctaw cultural heritage in the midst of enormous economic and social changes within the tribe have become a major goal.

The Oklahoma Choctaws, for example, have a language program that is available on the Internet. Instituted in 2000, the program has been a valuable tool in helping spread the

Located on tribal land near Philadelphia, Mississippi, Silver Star Resort & Casino, which opened in 1994, is part of the Pearl River Resort. In addition to Silver Star, the complex consists of Golden Moon Hotel & Casino; the 36-hole Dancing Rabbit Golf Club; a 285-acre lake; Geyser Falls, one of the largest water parks in the South; and campgrounds.

language, or "Chahta Anumpa," to people in Oklahoma and beyond. A number of former students have gone on to become teachers of the language in their communities. In addition, the One-Net program offers distance learning and reaches approximately forty high schools, two colleges, and any other interested persons with Internet access. In Bryan County (Oklahoma) Public Schools, the One-Net program meets the two-year "foreign language" requirement for secondary schools. The Oklahoma Choctaws also offer free language classes that are taught throughout Oklahoma and communities in Texas, Arkansas, and even California.

In 1997, the Mississippi Choctaws established the Tribal Language program, which set out to bring an end to the decline of the Choctaw language among Choctaw children. Surveys were first sent out to children to determine the kinds of services that were needed to maintain the language and in the fall of 1998, Roseanna L. Tubby-Nickey was named director. The objectives of the program are to immerse young Choctaw children in the language prior to entering kindergarten, teach high school children how to read and write the Choctaw language, and to purify the language, i.e., take mixed words (Choc-lish) out of the Choctaw vernacular. Some of the programs that have been implemented include working with Early Head Start programs to help children ages zero to two develop an understanding of Choctaw prior to entering school; a Choctaw Immersion Language Camp that is held each summer for children ages six to twelve; translation of written material into Choctaw; and annual language assessment tests for children.

The Oklahoma Choctaws are less closely settled and more spatially integrated into the overall population of southeastern Oklahoma than their tribal counterparts in Mississippi. Yet they, too, have been able to maintain their tribal identity and use government programs to foster economic development and promote the education, health, and social services within their nation. The U.S. government's policy of self-determination and the passage of the Indian Gaming Regulatory Act also helped the Oklahoma Choctaws to make tremendous strides during the last part of the twentieth century, which will almost certainly ensure future development in the twenty-first century.

Starting with the establishment of the Choctaw Bingo Parlor near Durant, the Oklahoma Choctaws launched themselves into an era of economic development and improvements in the delivery of education, health, and other services to their people. Besides the tribe's numerous travel plazas and smoke shops and gaming casinos, the Choctaws have worked diligently in recent years to diversify their economy. A tribute to this success is the fact that less than one-half of the tribe's revenue now comes from gaming.

To help foster new economic development, the Oklahoma Choctaws established the Choctaw Management/Services Enterprises (CM/SE) in 1997. CM/SE specializes in fulfilling scarce personnel requirements and providing information technology support services for document management of records that include scanning, filing, storage, retrieval and destruction of data, web development, systems analysis, statistical analysis, and database design, administration, and deployment. The main clients that use the service include the U.S. Department of Defense, the U.S. Army, Navy, and Air Force, and the Indian Health Service. CM/SE has numerous contracts with various governmental agencies and provides personnel at more than 215 sites in the United States and in 12 foreign countries.

In 1997, the Choctaws purchased an industrial park in Hugo, Oklahoma. One of the first businesses that was set up in the park was a trailer manufacturing plant. Other factories that build modular houses have also been established in Stigler and Coalgate. In addition, the Choctaw Manufacturing and Development Corporation (CMDC) has been instrumental in attracting other businesses and obtaining contracts from various governmental and private agencies. Some of the diverse products built by the various manufacturing plants include machines to purify water and items used by the military, such as Stinger Missile containers and other types of shipping and storage vessels, as well as the Army Space Heater (ASH).

A great deal of the Choctaw Nation's recent success can be attributed to Chief Gregory Pyle, who won more than eighty percent of the vote in the 1999 tribal election and ran unopposed in the 2003 election. Under the leadership of Chiefs Pyle, Gardner, and Roberts in Oklahoma and Chief Martin in Mississippi, both Choctaw groups have come to recognize that economic development is the cornerstone needed in order to improve the living standards of their people. And although several socioeconomic indicators reveal that the living conditions for Native Americans remains below the national norm, the leadership of the Mississippi and Oklahoma Choctaws have taken important steps to raise the standard of living of their respective groups. Tribal recognition and identity are now well secured, and future generations of Choctaws will be able to build upon a very firm foundation that today's Choctaws have begun to develop in recent years.

The Choctaws at a Glance

Tribe	Choctaw
Culture Area	Southeast
Original Geography	Gulf Coastal Plain
Linguistic Family	Muskogean
Current Population (2004)	40,404 (est.)—Choctaw Nation of Oklahoma 9,100 (est.)—Mississippi Choctaw
First European Contact	Hernando de Soto, Spanish, 1540
Federal Status	Recognized in Oklahoma. Reservation in Mississippi

1540   Choctaw Chief Tuscaloosa learns that Spanish explorer Hernando de Soto is approaching Choctaw territory; the Spaniards arrive on October 18 and leave November 14.

1699   The French establish a settlement at Fort Maurepas, on the coast of the Gulf of Mexico; Choctaw leaders meet with the French at Biloxi to discuss their mutual dislike of the English.

1702   The French found the settlement of Mobile; French leader Pierre LeMoyne d'Iberville holds a council at Mobile to try to form an alliance between the warring Choctaws and Chickasaws, in agreement with the French.

1703   Choctaws attack the Chickasaws.

1708   A peace agreement is made between Choctaws and Chickasaws.

1711   Fighting begins again between Choctaws and Chickasaws; Choctaws ally with England.

1715   Choctaws re-ally with the French.

1716   French Fort Rosalie is founded at present-day Natchez, Mississippi.

1718   French settlement of New Orleans is established.

1719   French Fort St. Pierre is founded on Yazoo River in Mississippi.

1720   Choctaws and French go to war with Chickasaws.

1720s   The French become involved in a war with the Natchez Indians.

1729   The Natchez storm Fort Rosalie and kill or capture the residents there; the French strike back the following year to rescue the prisoners, and by 1731, the Natchez are nearly annihilated.

1748   Civil war breaks out within Choctaw tribe.

1750   Civil war is settled by the Grandpré Treaty, in which the French impose harsh controls on the Choctaws.

1754   Choctaws threaten to ally with the English against the French.

1763 French and Indian War ends in French defeat; French colonial power comes to an end in America.

1765 Choctaws meet with the British at Mobile and sign a treaty defining the tribe's eastern border.

1775–1783 American Revolution is fought; some Choctaws serve as scouts for American troops fighting the British.

1783 Treaty of Paris ends the Revolution in a British defeat; British cede their American holdings south of Canada to the United States.

1786 On January 3, Choctaws sign the Treaty of Hopewell with the U.S. government; it establishes perpetual peace between them.

1792 Spanish sign a treaty of friendship with Choctaw, Cherokee, Chickasaw, and Creek tribes.

1795 After signing the Treaty of San Lorenzo (also known as Pinckney's Treaty), Spain removes its settlers from north of the 31st parallel of latitude, leaving the Choctaws on U.S.-controlled lands.

1798 Mississippi Territory is formed.

1801 Under the Treaty of Fort Adams, the U.S. government obtains more than two million acres of Choctaw territory and the right to construct a road from the town of Natchez to Nashville, Tennessee.

1802 Choctaws sign the Treaty of Fort Confederation, which redefines the tribe's eastern boundary and cedes more land to the U.S. government.

1803 Choctaws and the United States sign the Treaty of Hoe Buckintoopa, in which the U.S. government receives more than 850,000 acres of Choctaw territory in return for nominal payments to Choctaw chiefs; the United States purchases the Louisiana Territory from France.

1804 Congress passes the Louisiana Territorial Act, granting the president power to negotiate with Indian tribes for their removal.

1805   Under the Treaty of Mount Dexter, Choctaws give up more than four million acres in return for the U.S. government's agreement to pay off a debt the tribe owed to Panton, Leslie and Company.

1811   Shawnee leader Tecumseh travels to Choctaw lands to try to get the tribe's support to form an Indian confederacy in opposition to the United States; the tribe declines his offer.

1812–1814   Many Choctaws fight on the U.S. side in the War of 1812.

1813   Creek War against the United States begins; during the conflict, many Choctaws fight on the side of the United States.

1816   Under the Treaty of Fort St. Stephens, the Choctaws surrender approximately three million acres to the United States in a settlement following the Creek War.

1817   The western section of Mississippi Territory becomes the state of Mississippi.

1818   First school is founded in Choctaw territory; missionaries arrive in Choctaw lands.

1819   Spain officially cedes the territory of Florida to the United States.

1820   Generals Andrew Jackson and Thomas Hinds meet at Doak's Stand with Choctaw Chiefs Moshulatubbee, Pushmataha, and Apukshunnubbee; the Choctaws reluctantly agree to give up more than five million acres of their land in exchange for about thirteen million acres farther to the west.

1824   Choctaws send a delegation to Washington, D.C., to discuss problems stemming from the 1820 agreement made at Doak's Stand; Bureau of Indian Affairs (BIA) is established.

1825   On January 25, Choctaw Chief Moshulatubbee and Secretary of War John C. Calhoun sign the Treaty of 1825, redefining the Choctaws' eastern border in Indian Territory.

1829   The settlement of Skullyville is established by Choctaws in Indian Territory.

1830   Choctaws are granted Mississippi state citizenship; Choctaws and U.S. government negotiate a removal treaty; Choctaws are violently split over the proposal and some leave; the remaining leaders sign the Treaty of Dancing Rabbit Creek on September 27, giving up the remaining Choctaw land in Mississippi and agreeing to move to Indian Territory.

1831–1833   U.S. government schedules removal trips to Indian Territory for different groups of Choctaws.

1833   Choctaws invite the Chickasaws to settle in their nation, but the Chickasaws decline.

1834   Choctaws in Indian Territory hold their first tribal council meeting.

1837   Chickasaws sign the Treaty of Doaksville with Choctaws; under its terms, the Chickasaws agree to pay $530,000 for the right to settle in the Choctaw Nation.

1843   Choctaw council begins to fund boarding schools and Sunday schools.

1855   The Chickasaws, Choctaws, and United States sign the Treaty of 1855, which gives the Chickasaws the right to have their own tribal council for a district that becomes the Chickasaw Nation.

1861–1865   American Civil War is fought; Choctaws sign an alliance with the Confederacy and are ultimately defeated.

1866   Peace treaty signed with the U.S. government allows for the construction of a railroad across Choctaw territory.

1870–1872   The Missouri-Kansas-Texas Railroad builds a line through the Choctaw, Creek, and Cherokee Nations.

1879   David Folsom, a Choctaw who converted to Christianity, establishes a Baptist church for his fellow tribal members in Mississippi.

1887   Congress passes the General Allotment Act (called the Dawes Act), dividing up former tribal lands and parceling them out to individuals in small portions.

1889 Oklahoma Territory is organized from the western section of Indian Territory.

1893 Congress grants President Grover Cleveland the authority to form a committee, which became known as the Dawes Commission, to negotiate the termination of the Five Civilized Tribes' land titles.

1894 Dawes Commission approaches Choctaws; the tribe splits over the decision of whether or not to accept allotment.

1905 Choctaws send delegates to a conference of the Five Civilized Tribes to write a constitution for a separate state to be created from the lands of Indian Territory; Congress refuses to acknowledge the document.

1906 Choctaw tribal government is dissolved.

1907 Tribal rolls of those eligible to receive government allotments are closed; the Choctaws become citizens of the state of Oklahoma.

1908 Congress investigates conditions of the Mississippi Choctaws.

1916 Congress again performs an investigation into the conditions of the Mississippi Choctaws.

1918 The BIA establishes the Choctaw Indian Agency in Philadelphia, Mississippi.

1934 Indian Reorganization Act (also called the Wheeler-Howard Act) is passed by Congress; it prohibits further allotment of land and allows for the establishment of tribal governments.

1944 Secretary of the Interior announces the purchase of land that will become a reservation for the Mississippi Choctaws.

1953 Congress passes the so-called Termination Act, which tries to end the government's relationship with Indian tribes and encourage Indians to leave the reservations to move to urban areas.

1965 Choctaw Housing Authority is established.

1968 Congress passes the Indian Civil Rights Act.

1969 Choctaw leaders establish the Choctaw Development Enterprise.

1973 An industrial park is completed at Pearl River, Mississippi.

1975 The Choctaws adopt a revised constitution; Congress passes the Indian Self-Determination and Education Assistance Act.

1976 Mississippi Choctaws open the Choctaw Health Center.

1979 Phillip Martin elected chief of the Mississippi Band of Choctaw Indians.

1983 Oklahoma Choctaws adopt a modern constitution (it is ratified by the people the following year).

1987 Oklahoma Choctaws open the Choctaw Bingo Parlor.

1988 Congress passes the Indian Gaming Regulatory Act, requiring reservations to negotiate with states in order to have certain types of casino operations.

1994 Mississippi Choctaws open the Silver Star Resort and Casino.

1997 Oklahoma Choctaws buy an industrial park in Hugo; Gregory E. Pyle named chief of the Choctaw Nation.

1999 Pyle elected chief of the Choctaw Nation.

2000 Pearl River Resort opens in Choctaw, Mississippi.

2003 Pyle runs unopposed and is reelected chief of the Choctaw Nation.

agent—A person appointed by the Bureau of Indian Affairs to supervise U.S. government programs on a reservation and/or in a specific region; after 1908, the title "superintendent" was used instead of "agent."

alikchi—The Choctaw word for "medicine man" or "shaman." This person was in charge of conducting ceremonies to assure the success of hunting or war parties for the tribe.

allotment—U.S. policy, applied starting in 1887, to break up tribally owned reservations by assigning individual farms and ranches to Indians. It was intended as much to discourage traditional communal activities as to encourage private farming and to assimilate Indians into mainstream American life.

annuity—Compensation for land and/or resources based on terms of a treaty or other agreement between the United States and an individual tribe; consisted of goods, services, and cash given to the tribe every year for a specified period.

archaeology—The recovery and study of evidence of human ways of life, especially that of prehistoric peoples but also including that of historic peoples.

artifact—Any object made by human beings, such as a tool, garment, dwelling, or ornament.

Bureau of Indian Affairs (BIA)—A U.S. government agency established by the War Department in 1824 and assigned to the Department of the Interior in 1849. Originally intended to manage trade and other relations with Indians, the BIA now seeks to develop and implement programs to encourage Indians to manage their own affairs and to improve their educational opportunities and general social and economic well-being.

Choctaw—Indian tribe that traditionally lived in what is now Mississippi, western Alabama, and eastern Louisiana. Today, members of the Choctaw tribe also live in Oklahoma, Tennessee, Texas, California, and Washington.

clan—A multigenerational group having a shared identity, organization, and property, based on belief in their descent from a common ancestor. Because clan members consider themselves closely related, marriage within a clan is strictly prohibited.

culture—The learned behavior of humans; nonbiological, socially taught activities; the way of life of a group of people.

economic development—A process of creating wealth through the mobilization of human, financial, capital, physical, and natural resources to generate marketable goods and services.

Five Civilized Tribes—A loose confederation of the Creek, Choctaw, Chickasaw, Cherokee, and Seminole tribes, formed in 1859 to preserve Indian self-government in the face of a growing number of non-Indian settlers in Indian Territory. The word *civilized* referred to the adoption by these tribes of many non-Indian customs.

floodplain—Level land that is frequently submerged when rivers flood during the spring thaw. This flooding returns to the soil nutrients that are drained every year by cultivation.

Green Corn Dance—Celebration of purification, forgiveness, and thanksgiving held annually when the new crop of corn ripened.

Indian Reorganization Act (IRA)—The 1934 federal law that ended the policy of allotting plots of land to individuals and provided for political and economic development of reservation communities. The responsibilities of self-government were permitted, and tribes wrote their own constitutions for that purpose.

Indian Territory—An area in the south-central United States, including most of present-day Oklahoma, in which the U.S. government wanted to resettle Indians from other regions, especially from states east of the Mississippi River.

matrilineal; matrilineality—A principle of descent by which kinship is traced through female ancestors; the basis for Choctaw clan membership.

mingo—A Choctaw district chief.

mound—A large earthen construction built by prehistoric American Indians as a base for a public building or to contain human graves.

Nanih Waiya—A large mound sacred to the Choctaws and looked upon as their birthplace. Also the name given to the first council house in the Choctaw Nation in Indian Territory.

nation—A self-governing Indian group.

prehistory—Anything that happened before written records existed for a given locality. In North America, anything earlier than the first contact with Europeans is considered to be prehistoric.

removal policy—Federal policy, begun in 1830, calling for the sale of all Indian land in the eastern and southern United States and for the migration of Indians from these areas to lands across the Mississippi River. The Choctaws were the first tribe to be removed.

reservation; reserve—A tract of land set aside by treaty for Indian occupation and use.

self-determination—A policy that provides maximum Indian participation in the government and education of Indian people, and also provides full participation of Indian tribes in programs and services conducted by the federal government for Indians. Although initiated under President Lyndon Johnson, Congress did not enact the Indian Self-Determination and Education Assistance Act until 1975.

squatters—People who occupy property without having legal title to it.

tenant farmer—One who raises crops on land owned by another person and pays rent in cash or with a share of the crops.

termination—The removal of Indian tribes from federal government supervision and of Indian lands from federal trust status. The policy was initiated by Congress in the 1950s during the presidencies of Harry S. Truman and Dwight D. Eisenhower.

treaty—A contract negotiated between representatives of the United States or another national government and one or more Indian tribes. Treaties dealt with surrender of political independence, peaceful relations, terms of land sales, boundaries, and related matters.

tribe—A type of society consisting of several or many separate communities united by kinship and such social units as clans, religious organizations, and economic and political institutions. Tribes generally share a common culture and language, are characterized by economic and political equality, and thus lack social classes and authoritative chiefs.

trust—The relationship that exists between a guardian and a ward.

Baird, W. David. *The Choctaw People.* Phoenix, Ariz.: Indian Tribal Series, 1973.

Blanchard, Kendall. *The Mississippi Choctaw at Play: The Serious Side of Leisure.* Champaign, Ill.: University of Illinois Press, 1981.

Bounds, Thelma V. *Children of Nanih Waiya.* San Antonio, Tex: Naylor, 1964.

Carson, James Taylor. *Searching for the Bright Path: The Mississippi Choctaws from Prehistory to Removal.* Lincoln, Nebr.: University of Nebraska Press, 1999.

Debo, Angie. *The Rise and Fall of the Choctaw Republic,* 2nd ed. Norman, Okla.: University of Oklahoma Press, 1961.

DeRosier, Arthur H., Jr. *The Removal of the Choctaw Indians.* Knoxville, Tenn.: University of Tennessee Press, 1970.

Foreman, Grant. *The Five Civilized Tribes.* Norman, Okla.: University of Oklahoma Press, 1934.

Galloway, Patricia. *Choctaw Genesis 1500–1700.* Lincoln, Nebr.: University of Nebraska Press, 1995.

Kidwell, Clara Sue, and Charles Roberts. *The Choctaws: A Critical Bibliography.* Bloomington, Ind.: Indiana University Press for Newberry Library, 1980.

Lewis, Anna. *Chief Pushmataha, American Patriot: The Story of the Choctaws' Struggle for Survival.* New York: Exposition Press, 1959.

McKee, Jesse O., and Jon A. Schlenker. *The Choctaws: Cultural Evolution of a Native American Tribe.* Jackson, Miss.: University Press of Mississippi, 1980.

Milligan, James C. *The Choctaw of Oklahoma.* Abilene, Tex.: H.V. Chapman & Sons, 2003.

O'Brien, Greg. *Choctaws in a Revolutionary Age 1750–1830.* Lincoln, Nebr.: University of Nebraska Press, 2002.

Reeves, Carolyn Keller, ed. *The Choctaw before Removal.* Jackson, Miss.: University Press of Mississippi, 1985.

Wells, Mary Ann. *Native Land: Mississippi 1540–1798*. Jackson, Miss.: University Press of Mississippi, 1994.

Wells, Samuel J., and Roseanna Tubby, eds. *After Removal: The Choctaw in Mississippi*. Jackson, Miss.: University Press of Mississippi, 1986.

Websites

History of the Choctaws
http://www.ajourneypast.com/choctawhistory.html

Mississippi Band of Choctaws
http://www.choctaw.org

Choctaw Nation of Oklahoma
http://www.choctawnation.com

Mississippi Historical Society
http://mshistory.k12.ms.us/archives.html

PICTURE CREDITS

page:

3: Mississippi Department of
Archives and History

7: ©Hulton|Archive by
Getty Images

16: Library of Congress,
LC-USZC2-2257

25: ©Hulton|Archive by Getty Images

33: Archives and Manuscripts Division
of the Oklahoma Historical Society

38: © Michael Maslan Historic
Photographs/CORBIS

43: Archives and Manuscripts Division
of the Oklahoma Historical Society

50: © CORBIS

60: Western History Collections,
University of Oklahoma Library

64: Library of Congress

73: © Ed Kashi/CORBIS

83: Associated Press, AP/Rogelio Solis

85: Associated Press, AP/Rogelio Solis

A: Museum of the Red River, Oklahoma

B: Museum of the Red River, Oklahoma

C: Museum of the Red River, Oklahoma

D: Museum of the Red River, Oklahoma

E: Museum of the Red River, Oklahoma

F: Museum of the Red River, Oklahoma

G: Museum of the Red River, Oklahoma

H: Museum of the Red River, Oklahoma

Cover: Museum of the Red River, Oklahoma

Jesse O. McKee is professor emeritus of geography at the University of Southern Mississippi. He holds a B.S. degree from Clarion University of Pennsylvania and an M.A. and Ph.D. in geography from Michigan State University. He is coauthor of *The Choctaws: Cultural Evolution of a Native American Tribe,* coeditor of *Mississippi: A Sense of Place,* and editor of *Mississippi: Portrait of an American State* and *Ethnicity in Contemporary America: A Geographical Appraisal.* He has also authored several articles and book chapters on the Choctaws and other books and articles on various topics in cultural/historical geography. Among the many research grants Professor McKee has received are a Fulbright-Hays travel grant for geographic research in Cameroon and a Geographic Alliance grant from the National Geographic Society for the improvement of geographic education in public secondary schools.

Ada E. Deer is the director of the American Indian Studies program at the University of Wisconsin-Madison. She was the first woman to serve as chair of her tribe, the Menominee Nation, the first woman to head the Bureau of Indian Affairs in the U.S. Department of the Interior, and the first American Indian woman to run for Congress and secretary of state of Wisconsin. Deer has also chaired the Native American Rights Fund, coordinated workshops to train American Indian women as leaders, and championed Indian participation in the Peace Corps. She holds degrees in social work from Wisconsin and Columbia.